It's another great book from CGP...

This book is for anyone doing the **AQA Level 1/Level 2 Certificate in Chemistry**.

It's got clear, concise revision notes covering everything you'll need to do well in the exams. What's more, we've included a **free** Online Edition so that you can revise on a computer or tablet — wherever you are.

How to get your free Online Edition

Just go to **cgpbooks.co.uk/extras** and enter this code...

1284 8484 1669 2795

By the way, this code only works for one person. If somebody else has used this book before you, they might have already claimed the Online Edition.

CGP — still the best! ☺

Our sole aim here at CGP is to produce the highest quality books — carefully written, immaculately presented and dangerously close to being funny.

Then we work our socks off to get them out to you — at the cheapest possible prices.

Contents

The Scientific Process

How Science Works... 2
Your Data's Got To Be Good.................................. 3
Bias and Issues Created by Science...................... 4
Science Has Limits... 5
Designing Investigations 6
Collecting Data.. 8
Processing and Presenting Data 9
Presenting Data.. 10
Drawing Conclusions... 11
Planning and Evaluating Investigations................ 12

Section One — Fundamental Ideas in Chemistry

States of Matter 13
Movement of Particles 14
Atoms.. 15
Atoms and the Periodic Table 16
Atomic Mass and Isotopes 17
Electron Shells 18
Compounds... 19
Relative Formula Mass 20
Percentage by Mass and Empirical Formulae 21
Balancing Equations 22
Calculating Masses in Reactions.......................... 23
Percentage Yield and Reversible Reactions.......... 24
Revision Summary for Section One....................... 25

Section Two — Bonding and Structure

Compounds and Ionic Bonding 26
Ions and Ionic Compounds................................... 27
Covalent Bonding 28
More Covalent Bonding.. 29
Covalent Substances: Two Kinds......................... 30
Fullerenes and Nanoscience 31
Revision Summary for Section Two 32

Section Three — Air and Water

Air 33
Oxygen and Burning... 34
Air Pollution 35
Water Quality 36
Rust.. 38
Revision Summary for Section Three.................... 39

Section Four — The Periodic Table and Metals

More About The Periodic Table............................. 40
Group 1 — The Alkali Metals 41
Group 7 — The Halogens 42
Transition Elements 43
Reactions of Metals 44
The Reactivity Series 45
Getting Metals From Rocks................................... 46
Impacts of Extracting Metals 49
Metals 50
Alloys 51
Revision Summary for Section Four...................... 52

Section Five — Acids, Bases and Reaction Rates

Acids and Bases.. 53
Oxides, Hydroxides and Ammonia....................... 54
Titrations 55
Titration Calculations 56
Making Salts 57
Metal Carbonates and Limestone......................... 58
Rates of Reaction.. 59
Measuring Rates of Reaction................................ 60
Collision Theory.. 61
Collision Theory and Catalysts 62
Revision Summary for Section Five 63

Section Six — Crude Oil and Organic Chemistry

Crude Oil... 64
Properties and Uses of Crude Oil......................... 65
Environmental Problems 66
More Environmental Problems............................. 67
Cracking Crude Oil... 68
Alkenes and Ethanol 69
Polymers.. 70
More on Polymers 71
Alcohols 72
Carboxylic Acids 73
Esters... 74
Revision Summary for Section Six 75

Section Seven — Energy and Equilibria

Energy Transfer in Reactions 76
Energy Transfers and Reversible Reactions 77
Energy Level Diagrams 78
Bond Dissociation Energy 79
Measuring Energy Transfer 80
Equilibrium and Yield 81
The Haber Process 82
Revision Summary for Section Seven 83

Section Eight — Electrolysis and Analysis

Electrolysis 84
Electrolysis of Sodium Chloride Solution 85
Electrolysis of Aluminium and Electroplating 86
Tests for Positive Ions 87
Tests for Negative Ions 88
Separating Mixtures 89
Paper Chromatography 90
Instrumental Methods 91
Revision Summary for Section Eight 92

Index 93
Answers 94

Published by CGP

From original material by Richard Parsons.

Editors:
Jane Applegarth, Katherine Craig, Jane Ellingham, Mary Falkner, Ben Fletcher, Chris Lindle, Rachel Ward.

Contributors:
Mike Bossart, Paddy Gannon, Mike Thompson.

ISBN: 978 1 84762 448 2

With thanks to Charlotte Burrows and Jamie Sinclair for the proofreading.
With thanks to Laura Jakubowski for the copyright research.

Graph to show trend in atmospheric CO_2 concentration and global temperature on page 67 based on data by EPICA Community Members 2004 and Siegenthaler et al 2005.

Every effort has been made to locate copyright holders and obtain permission to reproduce sources. For those sources where it has been difficult to trace the originator of the work, we would be grateful for information. If any copyright holder would like us to make an amendment to the acknowledgements, please notify us and we will gladly update the book at the next reprint. Thank you.

Groovy website: www.cgpbooks.co.uk

Printed by Elanders Ltd, Newcastle upon Tyne.
Jolly bits of clipart from CorelDRAW®

Photocopying — it's dull, grey and sometimes a bit naughty. Luckily, it's dead cheap, easy and quick to order more copies of this book from CGP — just call us on 0870 750 1242. Phew!

Text, design, layout and original illustrations © Coordination Group Publications Ltd. (CGP) 2013
All rights reserved.

The Scientific Process

How Science Works

You need to know a few things about the scientific process. First up is how science works — or how a scientist's mad idea turns into a widely accepted theory.

Scientists Come Up with Hypotheses — Then Test Them

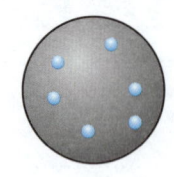

About 100 years ago, we thought atoms looked like this.

1) Scientists try to explain things. Everything.
2) They start by observing something they don't understand — it could be anything, e.g. planets in the sky, a person suffering from an illness, what matter is made of... anything.
3) Then, they come up with a hypothesis — a possible explanation for what they've observed. Scientists can sometimes form a model too — a simplified description or representation of what's physically going on.
4) The next step is to test whether the hypothesis might be right or not — this involves gathering evidence (i.e. data from investigations).
5) The scientist uses the hypothesis to make a prediction — a statement based on the hypothesis that can be tested. They then carry out an investigation.
6) If data from experiments or studies backs up the prediction, you're one step closer to figuring out if the hypothesis is true.

Investigations include lab experiments and studies.

Other Scientists Will Test the Hypothesis Too

1) Other scientists will use the hypothesis to make their own predictions, and carry out their own experiments or studies.
2) They'll also try to reproduce the original investigations to check the results.
3) And if all the experiments in the world back up the hypothesis, then scientists start to think it's true.
4) However, if a scientist somewhere in the world does an experiment that doesn't fit with the hypothesis (and other scientists can reproduce these results), then the hypothesis is in trouble.
5) When this happens, scientists have to come up with a new hypothesis (maybe a modification of the old hypothesis, or maybe a completely new one).

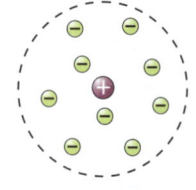

Then we thought they looked like this.

If Evidence Supports a Hypothesis, It's Accepted — for Now

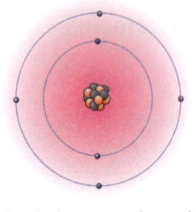

And then we thought they looked like this.

1) If pretty much every scientist in the world believes a hypothesis to be true because experiments back it up, then it usually goes in the textbooks for students to learn.
2) Accepted hypotheses are often referred to as theories.
3) Our currently accepted theories are the ones that have survived this 'trial by evidence' — they've been tested many, many times over the years and survived (while the less good ones have been ditched).
4) However... they never, never become hard and fast, totally indisputable fact. You can never know... it'd only take one odd, totally inexplicable result, and the hypothesising and testing would start all over again.

You expect me to believe that — then show me the evidence...

If scientists think something is true, they need to produce evidence to convince others — it's all part of testing a hypothesis. One hypothesis might survive these tests, while others won't — it's how things progress. And along the way some hypotheses will be disproved — i.e. shown not to be true.

The Scientific Process

Your Data's Got To Be Good

Evidence is the key to science — but not all evidence is equally good.
The way evidence is gathered can have a big effect on how trustworthy it is...

Lab Experiments and Studies Are Better Than Rumour

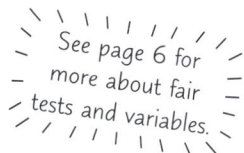
See page 6 for more about fair tests and variables.

1) Results from experiments in laboratories are great. A lab is the easiest place to control variables so that they're all kept constant (except for the one you're investigating). This makes it easier to carry out a FAIR TEST.

2) For things that you can't investigate in the lab (e.g. climate) you conduct scientific studies. As many of the variables as possible are controlled, to make it a fair test.

3) Old wives' tales, rumours, hearsay, "what someone said", and so on, should be taken with a pinch of salt. Without any evidence they're NOT scientific — they're just opinions.

The Bigger the Sample Size the Better

1) Data based on small samples isn't as good as data based on large samples. A sample should be representative of the whole population (i.e. it should share as many of the various characteristics in the population as possible) — a small sample can't do that as well.

2) The bigger the sample size the better, but scientists have to be realistic when choosing how big. For example, if you were studying the health effects of adding chlorine to drinking water it'd be great to study everyone in the UK (a huge sample), but it'd take ages and cost a bomb. Studying a thousand people would be more realistic.

Evidence Needs to be Repeatable and Reproducible

You can have confidence in the results if they can be repeated (during the same experiment) AND other scientists can reproduce them too (in other experiments). If the results aren't repeatable or reproducible, you can't believe them.

The data must be repeatable, and reproducible by others.

If the results are repeatable and reproducible, they're said to be reliable.

> **EXAMPLE:** In 1989, two scientists claimed that they'd produced 'cold fusion' (the energy source of the Sun — but without the big temperatures). It was huge news — if true, it would have meant free energy for the world... forever. However, other scientists just couldn't reproduce the results, so they couldn't be believed. And until they are, 'cold fusion' isn't going to be accepted as fact.

Evidence Also Needs to Be Valid

VALID means the data is repeatable, reproducible AND answers the original question.

> **EXAMPLE: DO POWER LINES CAUSE CANCER?**
> Some studies have found that children who live near overhead power lines are more likely to develop cancer. What they'd actually found was a correlation (relationship) between the variables "presence of power lines" and "incidence of cancer" — they found that as one changed, so did the other. But this evidence is not enough to say that the power lines cause cancer, as other explanations might be possible. For example, power lines are often near busy roads, so the areas tested could contain different levels of pollution from traffic. So these studies don't show a definite link and so don't answer the original question.

Repeat after me — repeatable and reproducible = great data...

By now you should have realised how important trustworthy evidence is (even more important than a good supply of spot cream). Unfortunately, you need to know loads more about fair tests and experiments — see pages 6-11.

The Scientific Process

Bias and Issues Created by Science

It isn't all hunky-dory in the world of science — there are some problems...

Scientific Evidence can be Presented in a Biased Way

1) People who want to make a point can sometimes present data in a biased way, e.g. they overemphasise a relationship in the data. (Sometimes without knowing they're doing it.)
2) And there are all sorts of reasons why people might want to do this — for example...

- They want to keep the organisation or company that's funding the research happy. (If the results aren't what they'd like they might not give them any more money to fund further research.)
- Governments might want to persuade voters, other governments, journalists, etc.
- Companies might want to 'big up' their products. Or make impressive safety claims.
- Environmental campaigners might want to persuade people to behave differently.

Things can Affect How Seriously Evidence is Taken

1) If an investigation is done by a team of highly-regarded scientists it's sometimes taken more seriously than evidence from less well known scientists.
2) But having experience, authority or a fancy qualification doesn't necessarily mean the evidence is good — the only way to tell is to look at the evidence scientifically (i.e. is it valid).
3) Also, some evidence might be ignored if it could create political problems, or emphasised if it helps a particular cause.

> **EXAMPLE:** Some governments were pretty slow to accept the fact that human activities are causing global warming, despite all the evidence. This is because accepting it means they've got to do something about it, which costs money and could hurt their economy. This could lose them a lot of votes.

Scientific Developments are Great, but they can Raise Issues

Scientific knowledge is increased by doing experiments. And this knowledge leads to scientific developments, e.g. new technologies or new advice. These developments can create issues though. For example:

Economic issues: Society can't always afford to do things scientists recommend (e.g. investing heavily in alternative energy sources) without cutting back elsewhere.

Social issues: Decisions based on scientific evidence affect people — e.g. should junk food be taxed more highly (to encourage people to eat healthily)? Should alcohol be banned (to prevent health problems)? Would the effect on people's lifestyles be acceptable...

Environmental issues: Chemical fertilisers may help us produce more food — but they also cause environmental problems.

Ethical issues: There are a lot of things that scientific developments have made possible, but should we do them? E.g. clone humans, develop better nuclear weapons.

Trust me — I've got a BSc, PhD, PC, TV and a DVD...

We all tend to swoon at people in authority, but you have to ignore that fact and look at the evidence (just because someone has got a whacking great list of letters after their name doesn't mean the evidence is good). Spotting biased evidence isn't the easiest thing in the world — ask yourself 'Does the scientist (or the person writing about it) stand to gain something (or lose something)?' If they do, it's possible that it could be biased.

The Scientific Process

Science Has Limits

Science can give us amazing things — cures for diseases, space travel, heated toilet seats...
But science has its limitations — there are questions that it just can't answer.

Some Questions Are Unanswered by Science — So Far

1) We don't understand everything. And we never will. We'll find out more, for sure — as more hypotheses are suggested, and more experiments are done. But there'll always be stuff we don't know.

   EXAMPLES:
   - Today we don't know as much as we'd like about the impacts of global warming.
     How much will sea level rise? And to what extent will weather patterns change?
   - We also don't know anywhere near as much as we'd like about the Universe.
     Are there other life forms out there? And what is the Universe made of?

2) These are complicated questions. At the moment scientists don't all agree on the answers because there isn't enough valid evidence.

3) But eventually, we probably will be able to answer these questions once and for all...
   All we need is more evidence.

4) But by then there'll be loads of new questions to answer.

Other Questions Are Unanswerable by Science

1) Then there's the other type... questions that all the experiments in the world won't help us answer — the "Should we be doing this at all?" type questions. There are always two sides...

2) Think about new drugs which can be taken to boost your 'brain power'.

3) Different people have different opinions.

> Some people think they're good... Or at least no worse than taking vitamins or eating oily fish. They could let you keep thinking for longer, or improve your memory. It's thought that new drugs could allow people to think in ways that are beyond the powers of normal brains — in effect, to become geniuses...
>
> Other people say they're bad... taking them would give you an unfair advantage in exams, say. And perhaps people would be pressured into taking them so that they could work more effectively, and for longer hours.

4) The question of whether something is morally or ethically right or wrong can't be answered by more experiments — there is no "right" or "wrong" answer.

5) The best we can do is get a consensus from society — a judgement that most people are more or less happy to live by. Science can provide more information to help people make this judgement, and the judgement might change over time. But in the end it's up to people and their conscience.

Chips or rice? — totally unanswerable by science...

Right — get this straight in your head — science can't tell you whether you should or shouldn't do something. That kind of thing is up to you and society to decide. There are tons of questions that science might be able to answer in the future — like how much sea level might rise due to global warming, what the Universe is made of and whatever happened to those pink stripy socks with Santa on that I used to have.

The Scientific Process

Designing Investigations

Real scientists need to know how to plan and carry out scientific experiments. Unluckily for you, those pesky examiners think you should be able to do the same — so you'll have questions on experiments in your exams. Don't worry though, these next seven pages have loads of information to help you out.

Investigations Produce Evidence to Support or Disprove a Hypothesis

1) Scientists observe things and come up with hypotheses to explain them (see page 2).
2) To figure out whether a hypothesis might be correct or not you need to do an investigation to gather some evidence.
3) The first step is to use the hypothesis to come up with a prediction — a statement about what you think will happen that you can test.
4) For example, if the hypothesis is:

   "Spots are caused by picking your nose too much."

   Then the prediction might be:

   "People who pick their nose more often will have more spots."

5) Investigations are used to see if there are patterns or relationships between two variables. For example, to see if there's a pattern or relationship between the variables 'having spots' and 'nose picking'.
6) The investigation has to be a FAIR TEST to make sure the evidence is valid...

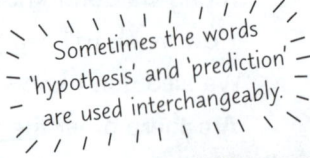
Sometimes the words 'hypothesis' and 'prediction' are used interchangeably.

See page 3 for more on validity.

To Make an Investigation a Fair Test You Have to Control the Variables

1) In a lab experiment you usually change one variable and measure how it affects the other variable.

   EXAMPLE: you might only change the temperature of a chemical reaction and measure how this affects the rate of reaction.

2) To make it a fair test everything else that could affect the results should stay the same (otherwise you can't tell if the thing you're changing is causing the results or not — the data won't be valid).

   EXAMPLE continued: you need to keep the concentration of the reactants the same, otherwise you won't know if any change in the rate of reaction is caused by the change in temperature, or a difference in reactant concentration.

3) The variable you CHANGE is called the INDEPENDENT variable.
4) The variable you MEASURE is called the DEPENDENT variable.
5) The variables that you KEEP THE SAME are called CONTROL variables.

   EXAMPLE continued:
   Independent variable = temperature
   Dependent variable = rate of reaction
   Control variables = volume of reactants, concentration of reactants etc.

6) Because you can't always control all the variables, you often need to use a CONTROL EXPERIMENT — an experiment that's kept under the same conditions as the rest of the investigation, but doesn't have anything done to it. This is so that you can see what happens when you don't change anything at all.

The Scientific Process

Designing Investigations

Trial Runs Help Figure out the Range and Interval of Variable Values

1) It's a good idea to do a trial run (preliminary experiment) first — a quick version of the experiment.

2) Trial runs are used to figure out the range of variable values used in the proper experiment (the upper and lower limit). If you don't get a change in the dependent variable at the lower values in the trial run, you might narrow the range in the proper experiment. But if you still get a big change at the lower values you might increase the range.

EXAMPLE continued:
You might do a trial run with a range of 10-50 °C. If there was no reaction at the lower end (e.g. 10-20 °C), you might narrow the range to 20-50 °C for the proper experiment.

If using 1 °C intervals doesn't give you much change in the rate of reaction each time you might decide to use 5 °C intervals, e.g. 20, 25, 30, 35, 40, 45 °C...

3) And trial runs can be used to figure out the interval (gaps) between the values too. The intervals can't be too small (otherwise the experiment would take ages), or too big (otherwise you might miss something).

4) Trial runs can also help you figure out whether or not your experiment is repeatable. E.g. if you repeat it three times and the results are all similar, the experiment is repeatable.

It Can Be Hard to Control the Variables in a Study

It's important that a study is a fair test, just like a lab experiment. It's a lot trickier to control the variables in a study than in a lab experiment though (see previous page). Sometimes you can't control them all, but you can use a control group to help. This is a group of whatever you're studying (people, plants, lemmings, etc.) that's kept under the same conditions as the group in the experiment, but doesn't have anything done to it.

EXAMPLE: If you're studying the effect of pesticides on crop growth, pesticide is applied to one field but not to another field (the control field). Both fields are planted with the same crop, and are in the same area (so they get the same weather conditions). The control field is there to try and account for variables like the weather, which don't stay the same all the time, but could affect the results.

Investigations Can be Hazardous

1) A hazard is something that can potentially cause harm. Hazards include:

- Microorganisms, e.g. some bacteria can make you ill.
- Chemicals, e.g. sulfuric acid can burn your skin and alcohols catch fire easily.
- Fire, e.g. an unattended Bunsen burner is a fire hazard.
- Electricity, e.g. faulty electrical equipment could give you a shock.

2) Scientists need to manage the risk of hazards by doing things to reduce them. For example:

- If you're working with sulfuric acid, always wear gloves and safety goggles. This will reduce the risk of the acid coming into contact with your skin and eyes.
- If you're using a Bunsen burner, stand it on a heat proof mat. This will reduce the risk of starting a fire.

You can find out about potential hazards by looking in textbooks, doing some internet research, or asking your teacher.

You won't get a trial run at the exam, so get learnin'...

All this info needs to be firmly lodged in your memory. Learn the names of the different variables — if you remember that the variable you chaNge is called the iNdependent variable, you can figure out the other ones.

The Scientific Process

Collecting Data

It's important to collect data that you can trust — data that's repeatable, reproducible, accurate and precise. Read on my intrepid friend...

Data Should be as Accurate and Precise as Possible

1) To show that results are repeatable, and so improve validity, readings should be repeated at least three times and a mean (average) calculated.
2) To make sure that results are reproducible you can cross check them by taking a second set of readings with another instrument (or a different observer).
3) Checking that results match with secondary sources, e.g. other studies, also increases the validity.
4) Data also needs to be ACCURATE. Really accurate results are really close to the true answer. The accuracy of the results usually depends on the method and the equipment used, e.g. when measuring the rate of a chemical reaction, you should use a stopwatch to accurately measure the time.
5) Data also needs to be PRECISE. Precise results are ones where the data is all really close to the mean (i.e. not spread out).

Remember — to be valid, data has to be repeatable and reproducible (p. 3).

The Equipment has to be Right for the Job

1) The measuring equipment used has to be sensitive enough to measure the changes being looked for. For example, if you need to measure changes of 1 ml you need to use a measuring cylinder that can measure in 1 ml steps — it'd be no good trying with one that only measures 10 ml steps.
2) The smallest change a measuring instrument can detect is called its RESOLUTION. E.g. some mass balances have a resolution of 1 g, some have a resolution of 0.1 g, and some are even more sensitive.
3) Also, equipment needs to be calibrated so that your data is more accurate. E.g. mass balances need to be set to zero before you start weighing things.

You Need to Look out for Errors and Anomalous Results

1) The results of an experiment will always vary a bit because of RANDOM ERRORS — tiny differences caused by things like human errors in measuring.
2) Their effect can be reduced by taking many readings and calculating the mean.
3) If the same error is made every time, it's called a SYSTEMATIC ERROR. For example, if you measured from the very end of your ruler instead of from the 0 cm mark every time, all your measurements would be a bit small.
4) Just to make things more complicated, if a systematic error is caused by using equipment that isn't zeroed properly it's called a ZERO ERROR. For example, if a mass balance always reads 1 gram before you put anything on it, all your measurements will be 1 gram too heavy.
5) Some systematic errors can be compensated for if you know about them though, e.g. if your mass balance always reads 1 gram before you put anything on it you can subtract 1 gram from all your results.
6) Sometimes you get a result that doesn't seem to fit in with the rest at all.
7) These results are called ANOMALOUS RESULTS.
8) They should be investigated to find out what caused them. If you can work out what happened (e.g. something was measured wrong) you can ignore them when processing the results.

Repeating the experiment in the exact same way and calculating an average won't correct a systematic error.

Park	No. of pigeons	No. of zebras
A	28	1
B	42	2
C	1127	0

Zero error — sounds like a Bruce Willis film...

Weirdly, data can be really precise but not very accurate, e.g. a fancy piece of lab equipment might give results that are precise, but if it's not calibrated properly those results won't be accurate.

The Scientific Process

Processing and Presenting Data

If you've got some results from an experiment, you might need to process and present them so you can look for patterns and relationships in them.

Data Needs to be Organised

1) Tables are dead useful for organising data.
2) If you have to draw a table use a ruler, make sure each column has a heading (including the units) and keep it neat and tidy.
3) You might be asked to describe the results in a table or pick out an anomalous result.
4) But tables aren't usually that great for showing patterns in data, so you might be asked to draw a graph.

You Might Have to Process Some Data

1) The repeats of an experiment should be used to calculate a mean (average). To do this ADD TOGETHER all the data values and DIVIDE by the total number of values in the sample.
2) You might also need to calculate the range (how spread out the data is). To do this find the LARGEST number and SUBTRACT the SMALLEST number from it.

Ignore anomalous results when calculating these.

EXAMPLE

Test tube	Repeat 1 (g)	Repeat 2 (g)	Repeat 3 (g)	Mean (g)	Range (g)
A	28	37	32	(28 + 37 + 32) ÷ 3 = 32.3	37 − 28 = 9
B	47	51	60	(47 + 51 + 60) ÷ 3 = 52.7	60 − 47 = 13
C	68	72	70	(68 + 72 + 70) ÷ 3 = 70.0	72 − 68 = 4

If the Data Comes in Categories, Present it in a Bar Chart

1) If either the independent or dependent variable is categoric (comes in distinct categories, e.g. blood types, metals) you should use a bar chart to display the data.
2) You also use them if one of the variables is discrete (the data can be counted in chunks, where there's no in-between value, e.g. number of people is discrete because you can't have half a person).
3) There are some golden rules you need to follow for drawing bar charts:

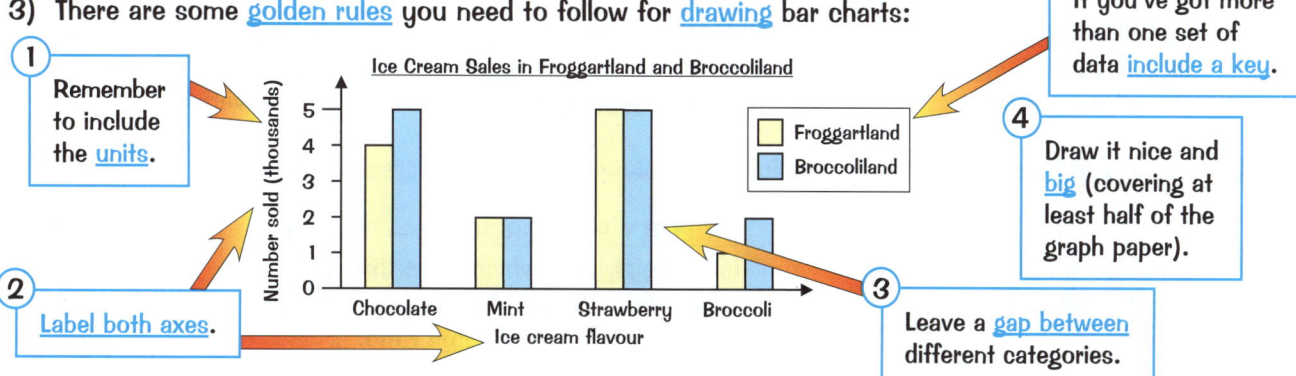

1. Remember to include the units.
2. Label both axes.
3. Leave a gap between different categories.
4. Draw it nice and big (covering at least half of the graph paper).
5. If you've got more than one set of data include a key.

Discrete variables love bar charts — although they'd never tell anyone that...

The stuff on this page might all seem a bit basic, but it's easy marks in the exams (which you'll kick yourself if you don't get). Examiners are a bit picky when it comes to bar charts — if you don't draw them properly they won't be happy. Also, double check any mean or range calculations you do, just to be sure they're correct.

The Scientific Process

Presenting Data

Scientists just <u>love</u> presenting data as <u>line graphs</u> (weirdos)...

If the Data is Continuous, Plot a Line Graph

1) If the independent and the dependent variable are <u>continuous</u> (numerical data that can have any value within a range, e.g. length, volume, temperature) you should use a <u>line graph</u> to display the data.

2) Here are the <u>rules</u> for <u>drawing</u> line graphs:

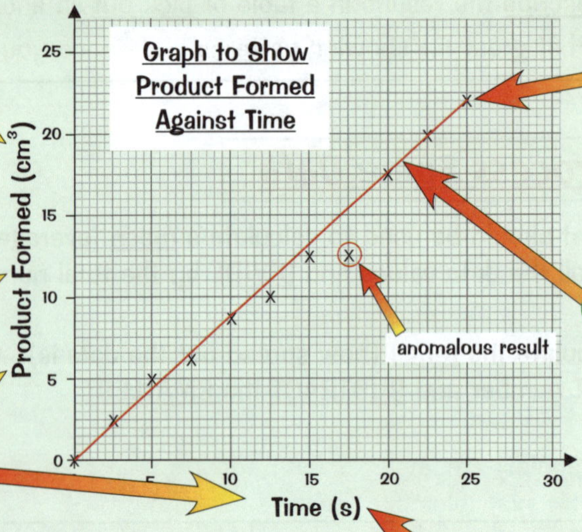

1 Remember to include the <u>units</u>.

2 Put the <u>dependent</u> variable (the thing you measure) on the <u>y-axis</u> (the <u>vertical</u> one).

3 <u>Label both axes</u>.

4 If you've got more than one set of data <u>include a key</u>.

5 Draw it nice and <u>big</u> (covering at least half of the graph paper).

6 Put the <u>independent</u> variable (the thing you change) on the <u>x-axis</u> (the <u>horizontal</u> one).

7 <u>Don't join the dots up</u>. You need to draw a <u>line of best fit</u> (or a <u>curve of best fit</u> if your points make a curve). When drawing a line (or curve), try to draw the line <u>through</u> or as <u>near</u> to <u>as many points as possible</u>, ignoring anomalous results.

8 To plot the points, use a <u>sharp pencil</u> and make a <u>neat little cross</u> (don't do blobs).

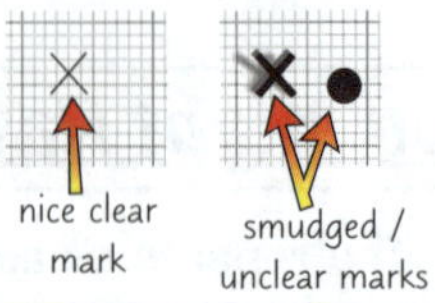

nice clear mark — smudged / unclear marks

(Graph to Show Product Formed Against Time — Product Formed (cm³) vs Time (s), with anomalous result labelled)

3) Line graphs are used to <u>show the relationship</u> between two variables (just like other graphs).

4) Data can show <u>three</u> different types of correlation (relationship):

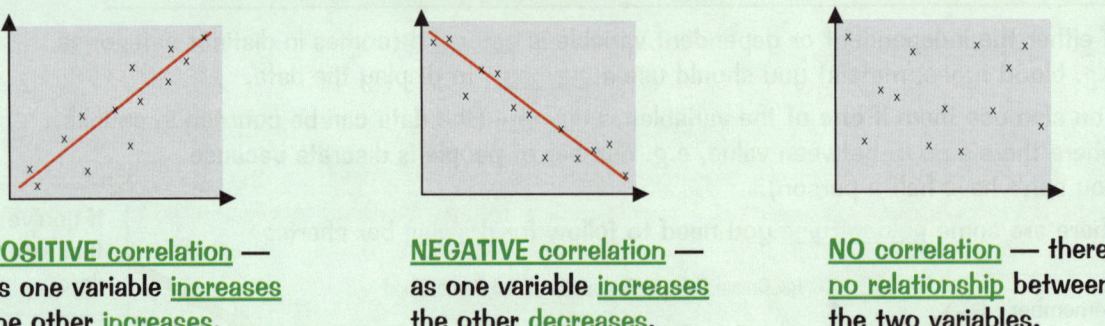

POSITIVE correlation — as one variable <u>increases</u> the other <u>increases</u>.

NEGATIVE correlation — as one variable <u>increases</u> the other <u>decreases</u>.

NO correlation — there's <u>no relationship</u> between the two variables.

5) You need to be able to describe the following relationships on line graphs too:

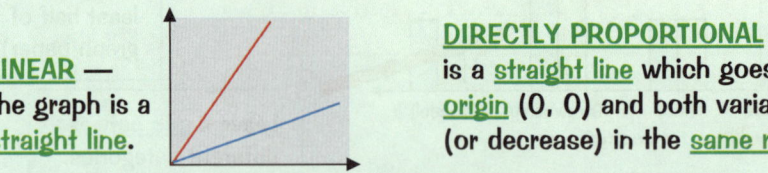

LINEAR — the graph is a <u>straight line</u>.

DIRECTLY PROPORTIONAL — the graph is a <u>straight line</u> which goes through the <u>origin</u> (0, 0) and both variables increase (or decrease) in the <u>same ratio</u>.

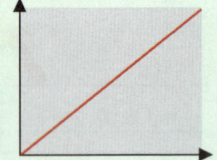

There's a positive correlation between revision and boredom...

...but there's also a positive correlation between <u>revision</u> and getting a <u>better mark in an exam</u>. Cover the page and write down the <u>eight things</u> you need to remember when <u>drawing line graphs</u>. No sneaky peeking either — I saw you.

The Scientific Process

Drawing Conclusions

Congratulations — you've made it to the fun part — drawing conclusions.

You Can Only Conclude What the Data Shows and NO MORE

1) Drawing conclusions might seem pretty straightforward — you just look at the data and say what pattern or relationship you see between the dependent and independent variables.

EXAMPLE: The table on the right shows the rate of a reaction in the presence of two different catalysts.

Catalyst	Rate of reaction (cm^3/s)
A	13.5
B	19.5
No catalyst	5.5

CONCLUSION: Catalyst B makes this reaction go faster than catalyst A.

2) But you've got to be really careful that your conclusion matches the data you've got and doesn't go any further.

EXAMPLE continued: You can't conclude that catalyst B increases the rate of any other reaction more than catalyst A — the results might be completely different.

3) You also need to be able to use the results to justify your conclusion (i.e. back up your conclusion with some specific data).

EXAMPLE continued: The rate of this reaction was 6 cm^3/s faster using catalyst B compared with catalyst A.

Correlation DOES NOT mean Cause

1) If two things are correlated (i.e. there's a relationship between them) it doesn't necessarily mean that a change in one variable is causing the change in the other — this is REALLY IMPORTANT, DON'T FORGET IT.

2) There are three possible reasons for a correlation:

① CHANCE

1) Even though it might seem a bit weird, it's possible that two things show a correlation in a study purely because of chance.

2) For example, one study might find a correlation between people's hair colour and how good they are at frisbee. But other scientists don't get a correlation when they investigate it — the results of the first study are just a fluke.

② LINKED BY A 3rd VARIABLE

1) A lot of the time it may look as if a change in one variable is causing a change in the other, but it isn't — a third variable links the two things.

2) For example, there's a correlation between water temperature and shark attacks. This obviously isn't because warmer water makes sharks crazy. Instead, they're linked by a third variable — the number of people swimming (more people swim when the water's hotter, and with more people in the water you get more shark attacks).

③ CAUSE

1) Sometimes a change in one variable does cause a change in the other.

2) For example, there's a correlation between smoking and lung cancer. This is because chemicals in tobacco smoke cause lung cancer.

3) You can only conclude that a correlation is due to cause when you've controlled all the variables that could, just could, be affecting the result. (For the smoking example above this would include things like age and exposure to other things that cause cancer).

I conclude that this page is a bit dull...

...yup, I lied at the start. Although, just because I find it dull doesn't mean that I can conclude it's dull (you might think it's the most interesting thing since that kid got his head stuck in the railings). In an exam you could be given a conclusion and asked whether the data supports it — so make sure you understand this page.

The Scientific Process

Planning and Evaluating Investigations

In an exam, you could be asked to plan or describe how you'd carry out an investigation. You might also be asked to say what you think of someone else's. Fear not, here's how you'd go about such things...

You Need to Be Able to Plan a Good Experiment

Here are some general tips on what to include when planning an experiment:
1) Say what you're measuring (i.e. what the dependent variable will be).
2) Say what you're changing (i.e. what the independent variable will be) and describe how you'll change it.
3) Describe the method and the apparatus you'd use (e.g. to measure the variables).
4) Describe what variables you're keeping constant — and how you're going to do it.
5) Say that you need to repeat the experiment three times, to make sure the results are repeatable.
6) Say whether you're using a control or not.

Here's an idea of the sort of thing you might be asked in an exam and what you might write as an answer...

Exam-style Question:

1 Describe an experiment to investigate the effect of acid concentration on the rate of reaction between dilute hydrochloric acid and magnesium metal.

Example Answer:

Set up a flask containing a measured mass of magnesium metal. Place the flask on a mass balance. Pour a measured volume of dilute hydrochloric acid into the flask and start the timer. Take readings of the mass at regular time intervals until the mass doesn't change anymore. The mass of gas lost from the reaction mixture can be calculated using this data.

Carry out the experiment again with different concentrations of dilute hydrochloric acid (e.g. 0.1 mol/dm³, 0.2 mol/dm³, 0.3 mol/dm³ and 0.4 mol/dm³).

The mass should be measured at the same time intervals for each acid concentration. The volume of acid should always be the same and the same mass of magnesium metal should be used each time. The temperature must also remain constant.

Repeat the experiment three times at each acid concentration and use the results to find the average mass of gas lost at each time interval for each concentration.

You could also collect the hydrogen in a gas syringe and measure its volume.

You Could Be Asked to Evaluate An Investigation

And finally — you might be asked to evaluate (assess) someone's investigation, data or conclusion. You need to think about the following things:
1) Method: Was it a fair test? Was the best method of data collection used?
2) Repeatability: Were enough repeat measurements taken? Were the repeated measurements similar?
3) Reproducibility: Are the results comparable to similar experiments done by other people?
4) Validity: Does the data answer the original question?

If the answer to all of these questions is a firm 'yes', you can have a good degree of confidence in the data and conclusion. If the answer to any of them is 'no' or 'umm, I don't know', then you might want to reconsider the data and conclusion. Have a think about how the investigation could be improved to get repeatable, reproducible and valid results.

Plan your way to exam success...

You might have to write a long, extended answer to any questions like this in an exam. Just remember to think about what you're going to say beforehand and in what order — that way you're less likely to forget something important. Like what it is you're actually measuring, or what the different variables are, say.

The Scientific Process

Section One — Fundamental Ideas in Chemistry

States of Matter

You can explain quite a bit of the stuff in Chemistry if you can get your head round this lot.

The Three States of Matter — Solid, Liquid and Gas

Materials come in three different forms — solid, liquid and gas. These are the Three States of Matter. Which state you get (solid, liquid or gas) depends on how strong the forces of attraction are between the particles of the material. How strong the forces are depends on THREE THINGS:
    a) the material   b) the temperature   c) the pressure.

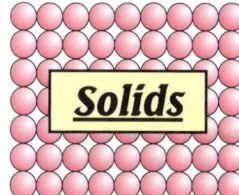
Solids

1) In solids, there are strong forces of attraction between particles, which holds them close together in fixed positions to form a very regular lattice arrangement.
2) The particles don't move from their positions, so all solids keep a definite shape and volume, and don't flow like liquids.
3) The particles vibrate about their positions — the hotter the solid becomes, the more they vibrate (causing solids to expand slightly when heated).

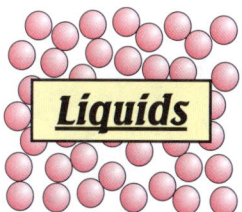
Liquids

1) In liquids, there is a weak force of attraction between particles. They're randomly arranged and free to move past each other, but they tend to stick closely together.
2) Liquids have a definite volume but don't keep a definite shape, and will flow to fill the bottom of a container.
3) The particles are constantly moving with random motion. The hotter the liquid gets, the faster they move. This causes liquids to expand slightly when heated.

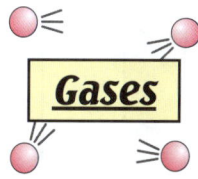
Gases

1) In gases, the force of attraction between the particles is very weak — they're free to move and are far apart. The particles in gases travel in straight lines.
2) Gases don't keep a definite shape or volume and will always fill any container.
3) The particles move constantly with random motion. The hotter the gas gets, the faster they move. Gases either expand when heated, or their pressure increases.

Substances Can Change from One State to Another

Physical changes don't change the particles — just their arrangement or their energy.

3) At a certain temperature, the particles have enough energy to break free from their positions. This is called MELTING and the solid turns into a liquid.

2) This makes the particles vibrate more, which weakens the forces that hold the solid together. This makes the solid expand.

1) When a solid is heated, its particles gain more energy.

4) When a liquid is heated, again the particles get even more energy.

5) This energy makes the particles move faster, which weakens and breaks the bonds holding the liquid together.

6) At a certain temperature, the particles have enough energy to break their bonds. This is called EVAPORATING and the liquid turns into a gas.

[Diagram: Solid ⇌ Liquid (melting/freezing) ⇌ Gas (evaporating/condensing); Solid → Gas (subliming)]

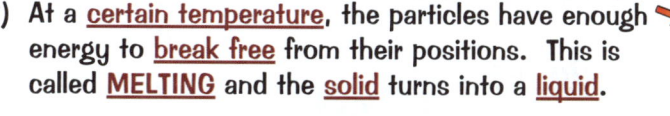

A Red Arrow means heat energy is supplied   A Blue Arrow means heat energy is given out

Phew, what a page — particle-ularly gripping stuff...

I think it's pretty clever the way you can explain all the differences between solids, liquids and gases with just a page full of blue and pink snooker balls. Anyway, that's the easy bit. The not-so-easy bit is learning it all.

Movement of Particles

There are many nifty experiments that you can do to observe the wonders of chemistry. Here are a few...

Particles Move Through Liquids and Gases (it's Called Diffusion)

Below are three experiments showing evidence for the existence of particles — they let you see diffusion. Diffusion is the gradual movement of particles from places where there are lots of them to places where there are fewer of them. It's just the natural tendency for particles of stuff to spread out.

Potassium Manganate(VII) and Water

Potassium manganate(VII) ($KMnO_4$) is great for this experiment because it's bright purple — so you can see the effect of the $KMnO_4$ particles moving through water.

1) If you take a beaker of water and place some potassium manganate(VII) at the bottom, the purple colour slowly spreads out to fill the beaker.
2) This shows the particles of potassium manganate(VII) are diffusing out among the particles of water.

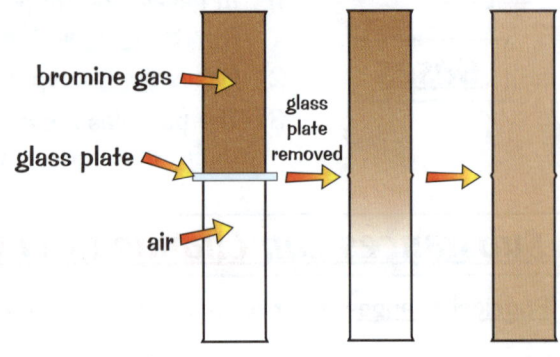

3) It's the random motion of particles in a liquid (see the previous page) that causes the purple colour to eventually be evenly spread out throughout the water.

Bromine Gas and Air

1) Bromine gas (Br_2) is a brown, strongly smelling gas. You can use it to show particles diffusing in gases.
2) Fill half a gas jar full of bromine gas, and the other half full of air — separate the gases with a glass plate.
3) When you remove the glass plate, you'll see the brown bromine gas slowly diffusing through the air.
4) The random motion of the particles means that the bromine will eventually diffuse right through the air.

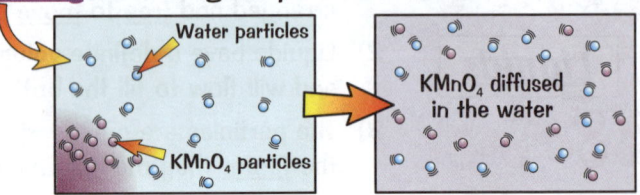

Ammonia and Hydrogen Chloride

1) Aqueous ammonia (NH_3) gives off ammonia gas. Hydrochloric acid (HCl) gives off hydrogen chloride gas.
2) If you set up an experiment like this...

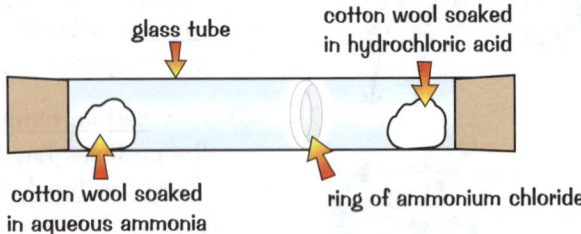

...you'll get a white ring of ammonium chloride forming in the glass tube.

3) The particles of NH_3 gas diffuse from one end of the tube and the particles of HCl gas diffuse from the other. When they meet they react to form particles of ammonium chloride.
4) The ring doesn't form exactly in the middle of the glass tube — it forms nearest the end of the tube where the hydrochloric acid was.
5) This is because the particles of ammonia are smaller and lighter than the particles of hydrogen chloride, so they diffuse through the air more quickly.

Sleeping on the book doesn't make the words diffuse into your head...

If you're lucky, you might get to see these experiments in the lab. Or, your teacher might show you some equally exciting but different experiments to demonstrate diffusion of particles. Either way, you've gotta learn it.

Section One — Fundamental Ideas in Chemistry

Atoms

Atoms are the building blocks of everything — and I mean everything.
They're amazingly tiny — you can only see them with an incredibly powerful microscope.

Atoms have a Small Nucleus Surrounded by Electrons

There are quite a few different (and equally useful) models of the atom — but chemists tend to like this nuclear model best. You can use it to explain pretty much the whole of Chemistry... which is nice.

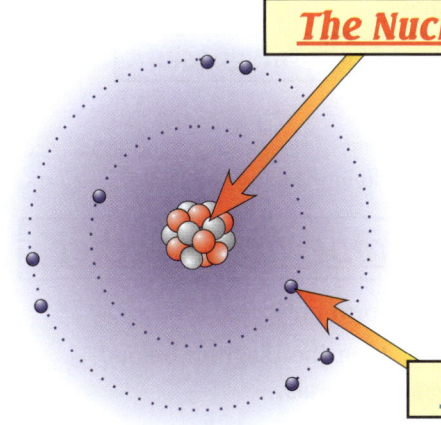

The Nucleus
1) It's in the middle of the atom.
2) It contains protons and neutrons.
3) Protons are positively charged.
4) Neutrons have the same mass as protons, but no charge (they're neutral).
5) So the nucleus has a positive charge overall because of the protons.
6) But size-wise it's tiny compared to the rest of the atom.

The Electrons
1) Move around the nucleus.
2) They're negatively charged.
3) They're tiny, with a very small mass compared to protons and neutrons, but they cover a lot of space.
4) They occupy shells around the nucleus.
5) These shells explain the whole of Chemistry.

Here's a summary of the different parts of an atom:

Particle	Relative mass	Relative charge
Proton	1	+1
Neutron	1	0
Electron	very small	-1

Number of Protons Equals Number of Electrons

1) Atoms have no electrical charge overall. They are neutral.
2) The charge on the electrons is the same size as the charge on the protons — but opposite.
3) This means the number of protons always equals the number of electrons in an atom.
4) If some electrons are added or removed, the atom becomes charged and is then an ion.

Elements Consist of One Type of Atom Only

1) Atoms can have different numbers of protons, neutrons and electrons. It's the number of protons in the nucleus that decides what type of atom it is.
2) For example, an atom with one proton in its nucleus is hydrogen and an atom with two protons is helium.
3) If a substance only contains one type of atom it's called an element:
4) There are about 100 different elements — quite a lot of everyday substances are elements.
5) So all the atoms of a particular element (e.g. nitrogen) have the same number of protons... and different elements have atoms with different numbers of protons.

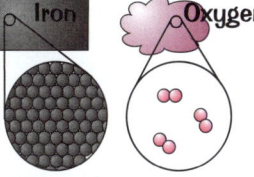

Number of protons = number of electrons...

This stuff might seem a bit useless at first, but it should be permanently engraved into your mind.
You need to know these basic facts — then you'll have a better chance of understanding the rest of Chemistry.

Section One — Fundamental Ideas in Chemistry

Atoms and the Periodic Table

Chemistry would be really messy if it was all big lists of names and properties. So instead they've come up with a kind of shorthand for the names, and made a beautiful table to organise the elements — like a big filing system. Might not be much fun, but it makes life (and exam questions) much, much easier.

Atoms Can be Represented by Symbols

Atoms of each element can be represented by a one or two letter symbol — it's a type of shorthand that saves you the bother of having to write the full name of the element.

Some make perfect sense, e.g.   C = carbon   O = oxygen   Mg = magnesium

Others seem to make about as much sense as an apple with a handle.

E.g.   Na = sodium   Fe = iron   Pb = lead

Most of these odd symbols actually come from the Latin names of the elements.

The Periodic Table Puts Elements with Similar Properties Together

1) The periodic table is laid out so that elements with similar properties form columns.
2) These vertical columns are called groups. Each group has a number (see the diagram below), and you might sometimes see the group numbers written as Roman numerals.
3) All of the elements in a group have the same number of electrons in their outer shell.
4) This is why elements in the same group have similar properties. So, if you know the properties of one element, you can predict properties of other elements in that group.
5) For example, the Group 1 elements are Li, Na, K, Rb, Cs and Fr. They're all metals and they react the same way. E.g. they all react with water to form an alkaline solution and hydrogen gas, and they all react with oxygen to form an oxide.
6) The elements in the final column (Group 0) are the noble gases. They all have eight electrons in their outer shell, apart from helium (which has two) — see page 18. This means they're stable and unreactive.

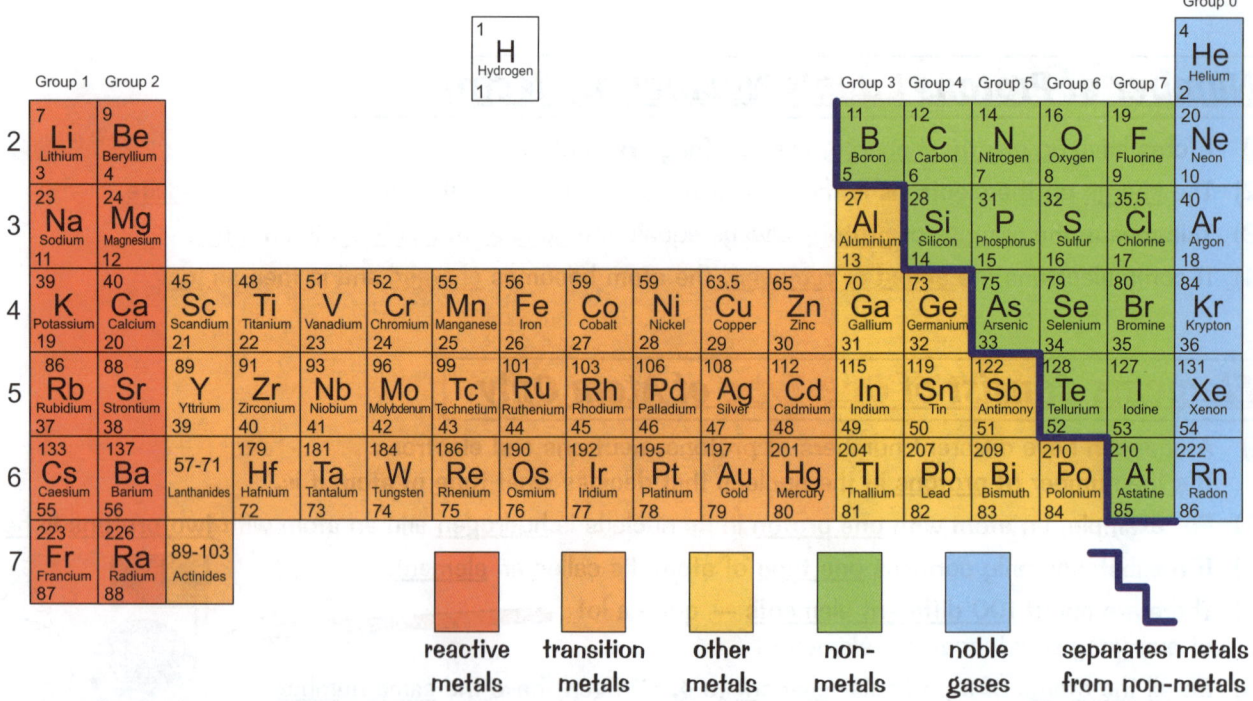

I'm in a chemistry band — I play the symbols...

Scientists keep making new elements and feeling well chuffed with themselves. The trouble is, these new elements only last for a fraction of a second before falling apart. You don't need to know the properties of each group of the periodic table, but if you're told, for example, that fluorine (Group 7) forms two-atom molecules, it's a fair guess that chlorine, bromine, iodine and astatine do too.

Section One — Fundamental Ideas in Chemistry

Atomic Mass and Isotopes

The main trouble you'll have with atomic number, mass number and relative atomic mass is probably remembering which one is which. But it'll be a lot easier once you understand what each term means.

Atomic Number and Mass Number Describe an Atom

These two numbers tell you how many of each kind of particle an atom has.

The Mass Number → $^{23}_{11}$Na
This is the total number of protons and neutrons.

The Atomic Number →
This is the number of protons, which conveniently also tells you the number of electrons.

1) The atomic number tells you how many protons there are.
2) Atoms of the same element all have the same number of protons — so atoms of different elements will have different numbers of protons.

So, if you want to find the number of neutrons in an atom, just subtract the atomic number from the mass number.

Isotopes Are the Same Except for an Extra Neutron or Two

A favourite exam question: "Explain what is meant by the term isotope". LEARN the definition:

> **Isotopes are: different atomic forms of the same element, which have the SAME number of PROTONS but a DIFFERENT number of NEUTRONS.**

1) The upshot is: isotopes must have the same atomic number but different mass numbers.
2) If they had different atomic numbers, they'd be different elements altogether.
3) Carbon-12 and carbon-14 are a very popular pair of isotopes.

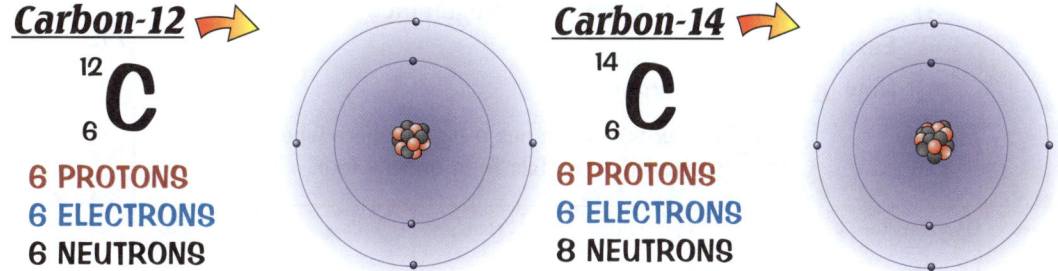

Carbon-12 → $^{12}_{6}$C
6 PROTONS
6 ELECTRONS
6 NEUTRONS

Carbon-14 → $^{14}_{6}$C
6 PROTONS
6 ELECTRONS
8 NEUTRONS

Relative Atomic Mass, A_r — Often the Same as Mass Number

1) This is just a way of saying how heavy different atoms are compared with the mass of an atom of carbon-12. So carbon-12 has A_r of exactly 12.
2) It turns out that the relative atomic mass A_r is usually just the same as the mass number of the element.

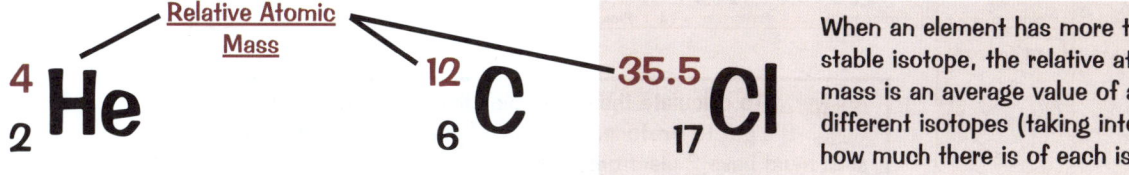

Relative Atomic Mass — $^{4}_{2}$He $^{12}_{6}$C $^{35.5}_{17}$Cl

When an element has more than one stable isotope, the relative atomic mass is an average value of all the different isotopes (taking into account how much there is of each isotope).

Helium has A_r = 4.   Carbon has A_r = 12.   Chlorine has A_r = 35.5.

Will this be in your exam — isotope so...

...because obviously you'll know it as well as you know not to eat yellow snow. Anyway... it's really important you understand that an isotope is just a slight variation on the same element. Not so crazy really.

Section One — Fundamental Ideas in Chemistry

Electron Shells

The fact that electrons occupy "shells" around the nucleus is what causes the whole of chemistry. Remember that, and watch how it applies to each bit of it. It's ace.

Electron Shell Rules:

1) Electrons always occupy shells (sometimes called energy levels).
2) The lowest energy levels are always filled first — these are the ones closest to the nucleus.
3) Only a certain number of electrons are allowed in each shell:
   1st shell: 2   2nd shell: 8   3rd shell: 8
4) Atoms are much happier when they have full electron shells — like the noble gases in Group 0.
5) In most atoms the outer shell is not full and this makes the atom want to react to fill it.

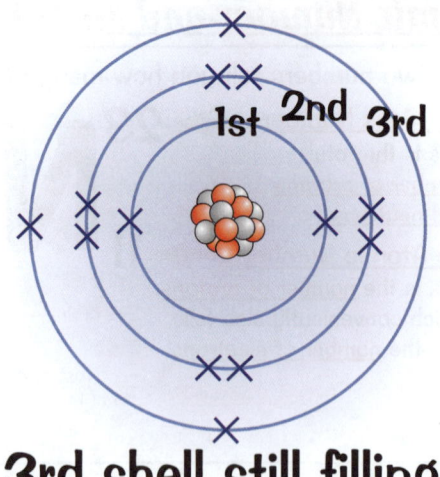

3rd shell still filling

Follow the Rules to Work Out Electronic Structures

You need to know the electronic structures for the first 20 elements (things get a bit more complicated after that). But they're not hard to work out. For a quick example, take nitrogen. Follow the steps...

1) The periodic table tells us nitrogen has seven protons... so it must have seven electrons.
2) Follow the 'Electron Shell Rules' above. The first shell can only take 2 electrons and the second shell can take a maximum of 8 electrons.
3) So the electronic structure for nitrogen must be 2, 5. Easy peasy.
4) Now you try it for argon.

The periodic table has a big gap here where the transition metals fit in on row four.

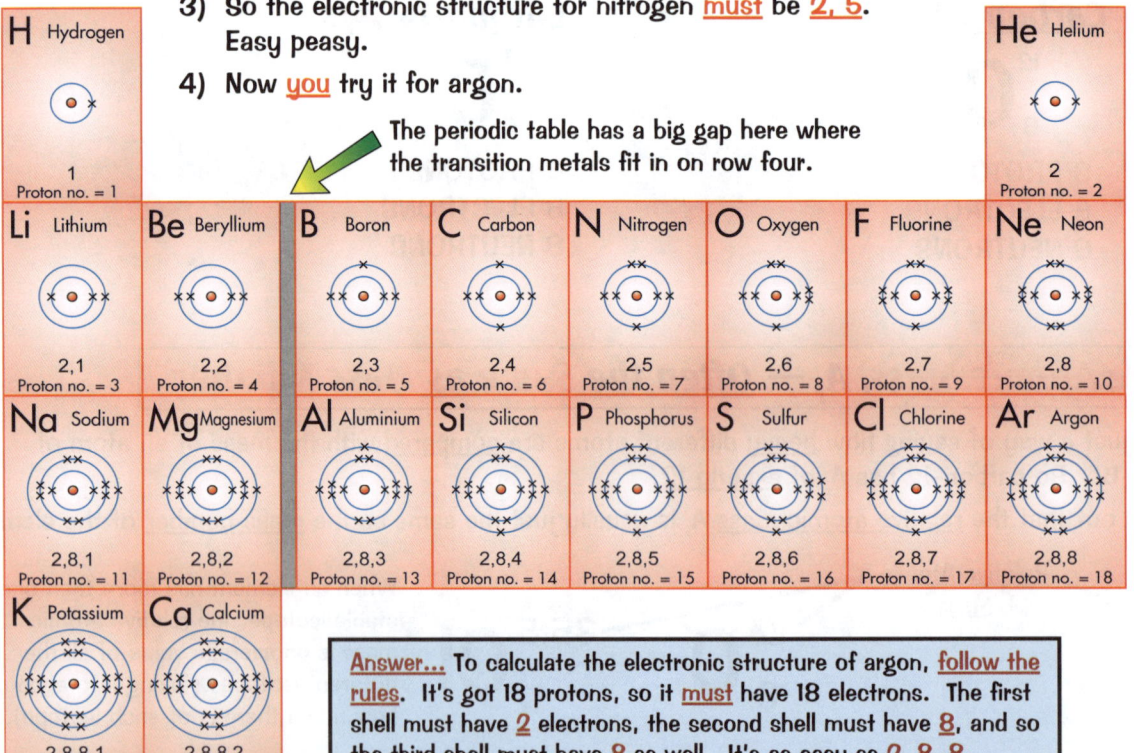

Answer... To calculate the electronic structure of argon, follow the rules. It's got 18 protons, so it must have 18 electrons. The first shell must have 2 electrons, the second shell must have 8, and so the third shell must have 8 as well. It's as easy as 2, 8, 8.

One little duck and two fat ladies — 2, 8, 8...

You need to know enough about electron shells to draw out that whole diagram at the bottom of the page without looking at it. Obviously, you don't have to learn each element separately, just learn the pattern. Cover the page: using a periodic table, find the atom with the electron structure 2, 8, 6.

Section One — Fundamental Ideas in Chemistry

Compounds

Life'd be oh so simple if you only had to worry about elements, even if there are a hundred or so of them. But you can mix and match elements to make lots of compounds, which complicates things no end.

Atoms Join Together to Make Compounds

1) When different elements react, atoms form chemical bonds with other atoms to form compounds. It's usually difficult to separate the two original elements out again.

2) Making bonds involves atoms giving away, taking or sharing electrons from their outer shells. Only the electrons are involved — it's nothing to do with the nuclei of the atoms at all.

3) A compound which is formed from a metal and a non-metal consists of ions.

- The metal atoms lose electrons to form positive ions.
- The non-metal atoms gain electrons to form negative ions.
- The opposite charges (positive and negative) of the ions mean that they're strongly attracted to each other. This is called IONIC bonding (see page 26). E.g. NaCl
- The ions that form have full outer electron shells. So they end up with the electron arrangement of the nearest noble gas (group 0 element — see page 16).

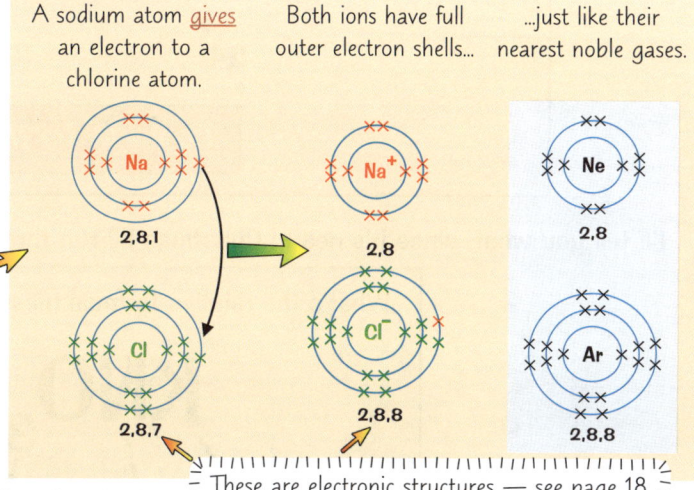

These are electronic structures — see page 18.

4) A compound formed from non-metals consists of molecules.

- Each atom shares an electron with another atom — this is called a COVALENT bond (see page 28).
- Each atom has to make enough covalent bonds to fill up its outer shell. E.g. HCl
- So the atoms end up with the electron arrangement of the nearest noble gas.

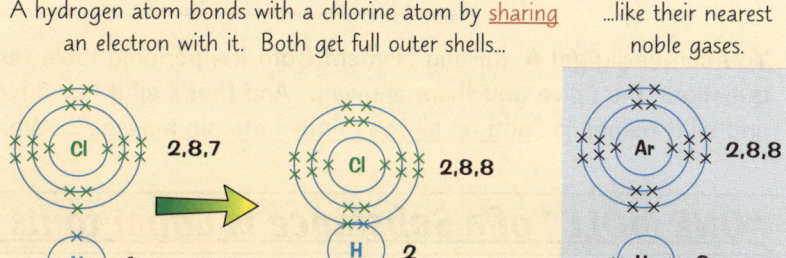

A Formula Shows What Atoms are in a Compound

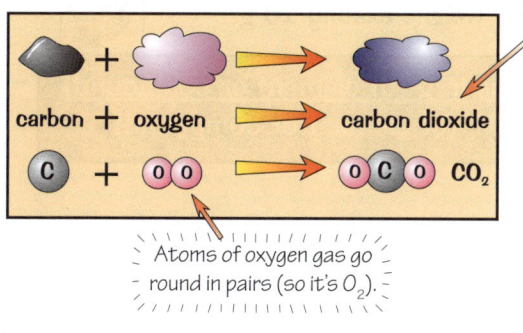

Atoms of oxygen gas go round in pairs (so it's O_2).

1) Carbon dioxide, CO_2, is a compound formed from a chemical reaction between carbon and oxygen. It contains 1 carbon atom and 2 oxygen atoms.

2) Here's another example: the formula of sulfuric acid is H_2SO_4. So, each molecule contains 2 hydrogen atoms, 1 sulfur atom and 4 oxygen atoms.

3) There might be brackets in a formula, e.g. calcium hydroxide is $Ca(OH)_2$. The little number outside the bracket applies to everything inside the brackets. So in $Ca(OH)_2$ there is 1 calcium atom, 2 oxygen atoms and 2 hydrogen atoms.

Not learning this stuff will only compound your problems...

So, atoms can be very caring and sharing little things when it comes to forming compounds. Some people could learn from them. Anyway, make sure you understand what compounds are and what the difference is between covalent and ionic bonding. It'll come in incredibly useful later on in your chemistry learnings. I promise.

Relative Formula Mass

The biggest trouble with relative formula mass is that it sounds so blood-curdling. It's very important though, so take a few deep breaths, and just enjoy, as the mists slowly clear...

Relative Formula Mass, M_r — Easy Peasy

If you have a compound like $MgCl_2$ then it has a relative formula mass, M_r, which is just all the relative atomic masses of the atoms it contains added together.

Relative atomic mass is usually just the same as the mass number of the element — see page 17.

For $MgCl_2$ it would be:

$MgCl_2$

$24 + (35.5 \times 2) = 95$

So the M_r for $MgCl_2$ is simply 95.

I'll tell you what, since it's nearly Christmas I'll run through another example for you:

What's the relative formula mass of KNO_3?

KNO_3

$39 + 14 + (16 \times 3) = 101$

So the M_r for KNO_3 is 101.

You can easily get A_r for any element from the periodic table (see inside front cover), but in a lot of questions they give you them anyway. And that's all it is. A big fancy name like relative formula mass and all it means is "add up all the relative atomic masses". What a swizz, eh?

"ONE MOLE" of a Substance is Equal to its M_r in Grams

The relative formula mass (A_r or M_r) of a substance in grams is known as one mole of that substance.

Examples:
Iron has an A_r of 56.   So one mole of iron weighs exactly 56 g
Nitrogen gas, N_2, has an M_r of 28 (2×14).   So one mole of N_2 weighs exactly 28 g

You can convert between moles and grams using this formula:

NUMBER OF MOLES = Mass in g (of element or compound) / M_r (of element or compound)

Example 1: How many moles are there in 42 g of carbon?
Answer: No. of moles = Mass (g) / M_r = 42/12 = 3.5 moles   Easy Peasy

Example 2: What is the mass of 125 moles of O_2?
Answer: No. of moles = Mass (g) / M_r so $125 = $ Mass (g) / (16×2)
$125 \times (16 \times 2) = $ Mass (g) $ = $ 4 000 g   Not Too Horrible

Numbers? — and you thought you were doing chemistry...

Learn the definitions of relative atomic mass and relative formula mass, then have a go at these:
1) Use the periodic table to find the relative atomic mass of these elements: Cu, K, Kr, Cl
2) Find the relative formula mass of: NaOH, Fe_2O_3, C_6H_{14}, $Mg(NO_3)_2$ Answers on page 94.

Section One — Fundamental Ideas in Chemistry

Percentage by Mass and Empirical Formulae

Although relative atomic mass and relative formula mass are _easy enough_, it can get just a tad _trickier_ when you start getting into other calculations which use them. It depends on how good your maths is basically, because it's all to do with ratios and percentages.

Calculating % Mass of an Element in a Compound

This is actually dead easy — so long as you've learnt this formula:

$$\text{Percentage mass OF AN ELEMENT IN A COMPOUND} = \frac{A_r \times \text{No. of atoms (of that element)}}{M_r \text{ (of whole compound)}} \times 100$$

If you don't learn the formula then you'd better be pretty smart — or you'll struggle.

EXAMPLE: Find the percentage mass of sodium in sodium carbonate, Na_2CO_3.

ANSWER:
A_r of sodium = 23, A_r of carbon = 12, A_r of oxygen = 16
M_r of Na_2CO_3 = (2 × 23) + 12 + (3 × 16) = 106

Now use the formula:

$$\underline{\text{Percentage mass}} = \frac{A_r \times n}{M_r} \times 100 = \frac{23 \times 2}{106} \times 100 = 43.4\%$$

And there you have it. Sodium makes up _43.4%_ of the mass of sodium carbonate.

Finding the Empirical Formula (from Masses or Percentages)

This also sounds a lot worse than it really is. Try this for an easy peasy stepwise method:

1) List all the elements in the compound (there's usually only two or three!)
2) Underneath them, write their experimental masses or percentages.
3) Divide each mass or percentage by the A_r for that particular element.
4) Turn the numbers you get into a nice simple ratio by multiplying and/or dividing them by well-chosen numbers.
5) Get the ratio in its simplest form, and that tells you the empirical formula of the compound.

Example: Find the empirical formula of the iron oxide produced when 44.8 g of iron react with 19.2 g of oxygen. (A_r for iron = 56, A_r for oxygen = 16)

Method:

		Fe	O
1)	List the two elements:	Fe	O
2)	Write in the experimental masses:	44.8	19.2
3)	Divide by the A_r for each element:	$44.8/56 = 0.8$	$19.2/16 = 1.2$
4)	Multiply by 10...	8	12
	...then divide by 4:	2	3

5) So the simplest formula is 2 atoms of Fe to 3 atoms of O, i.e. Fe_2O_3. And that's it done.

> You need to realise (for the exam) that this empirical method (i.e. based on experiment) is the only way of finding out the formula of a compound. Rust is iron oxide, sure, but is it FeO, or Fe_2O_3? Only an experiment to determine the empirical formula will tell you for certain.

With this empirical formula I can rule the world! — mwa ha ha ha...

Make sure you learn the formula and the five steps in the red box. Then try these: Answers on page 94.
1) Find the percentage mass of oxygen in each of these: a) Fe_2O_3 b) H_2O c) $CaCO_3$ d) H_2SO_4.
2) Find the empirical formula of the compound formed from 2.4 g of carbon and 0.8 g of hydrogen.

Section One — Fundamental Ideas in Chemistry

Balancing Equations

<u>Equations need a lot of practice</u> if you're going to get them right — don't just <u>skate</u> over this stuff.

Equations Show the Reactants and Products of a Reaction

1) A chemical reaction can be described as the process of going from <u>reactants</u> to <u>products</u>. You can write <u>word equations</u> or <u>symbol equations</u> to show any chemical reaction.

   e.g. magnesium reacts with oxygen to produce magnesium oxide:

Word equation:	magnesium + oxygen → magnesium oxide
Balanced symbol equation:	$2Mg + O_2 → 2MgO$

2) Atoms <u>aren't lost or made</u> in chemical reactions. You still have the <u>same atoms</u> at the <u>end</u> as you had at the <u>start</u>. They're just <u>arranged</u> in different ways.

3) Because atoms don't just appear or disappear, the mass of the reactants <u>equals</u> the mass of the products. So, if you completely react <u>6 g of magnesium</u> with <u>4 g of oxygen</u>, you'd get <u>10 g of magnesium oxide</u>.

Look out for <u>state symbols</u> in equations — they tell you what <u>physical state</u> the reactants and products are in:

(s) — Solid	(l) — Liquid	(g) — Gas	(aq) — Aqueous (dissolved in water)

Here's the example with the state symbols in: $2Mg(s) + O_2(g) → 2MgO(s)$

So, this is solid magnesium reacting with oxygen gas to make solid magnesium oxide.

Balancing the Equation — Match Them Up One by One

1) There must always be the <u>same</u> number of atoms of each element on <u>both sides</u> — they can't just <u>disappear</u>.

2) You <u>balance</u> the equation by putting numbers <u>in front</u> of the formulas where needed. Take this equation for reacting sulfuric acid (H_2SO_4) with sodium hydroxide (NaOH) to get sodium sulfate (Na_2SO_4) and water (H_2O):

$$H_2SO_4 + NaOH → Na_2SO_4 + H_2O$$

The <u>formulas</u> are all correct but the numbers of some atoms <u>don't match up</u> on both sides. E.g. there are 3 Hs on the left, but only 2 on the right. You <u>can't change formulas</u> like H_2O to H_3O. You can only put numbers <u>in front of them</u>:

Method: Balance Just ONE Type of Atom at a Time

1) Find an element that <u>doesn't balance</u> and <u>pencil in a number</u> to try and sort it out.
2) <u>See where it gets you</u>. It may create <u>another imbalance</u> — if so, just pencil in <u>another number</u> and see where that gets you.
3) Carry on chasing <u>unbalanced</u> elements and it'll <u>sort itself out</u> pretty quickly.

<u>I'll show you</u>. In the equation above you soon notice we're short of H atoms on the RHS (Right-Hand Side).

1) The only thing you can do about that is make it $2H_2O$ instead of just H_2O:

$$H_2SO_4 + NaOH → Na_2SO_4 + 2H_2O$$

2) But that now causes too many H atoms and O atoms on the RHS, so to balance that up you could try putting 2NaOH on the LHS (Left-Hand Side):

$$H_2SO_4 + 2NaOH → Na_2SO_4 + 2H_2O$$

3) And suddenly there it is! <u>Everything balances</u>. And you'll notice the Na just sorted itself out.

Balanced diet — a biscuit in one hand, an apple in the other...

Balance these symbol equations*: 1) $Fe_2O_3 + H_2 → Fe + H_2O$ 2) $HCl + Al → AlCl_3 + H_2$

*Answers on page 94.

Calculating Masses in Reactions

These can be kinda scary too, but chill out, little trembling one — just relax and enjoy.

The Three Important Steps — *Not to Be Missed...*

(Miss one out and it'll all go horribly wrong, believe me.)

> 1) <u>Write out</u> the balanced <u>equation</u>
> 2) <u>Work out</u> M_r — just for the <u>two bits you want</u>
> 3) Apply the rule: <u>Divide to get one, then multiply to get all</u>
>   (But you have to apply this first to the substance they give you information about, and then the other one!)

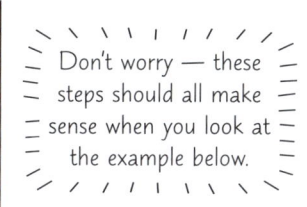

Don't worry — these steps should all make sense when you look at the example below.

Example: What mass of magnesium oxide is produced when 60 g of magnesium is burned in air?

Answer:

1) Write out the <u>balanced equation</u>: $2Mg + O_2 \rightarrow 2MgO$

2) Work out the <u>relative formula masses</u>:
   (don't do the oxygen — we don't need it)
   $$2 \times 24 \rightarrow 2 \times (24+16)$$
   $$48 \rightarrow 80$$

3) Apply the rule: <u>Divide to get one, then multiply to get all</u>:
   The two numbers, 48 and 80, tell us that <u>48 g of Mg react to give 80 g of MgO</u>.
   Here's the tricky bit. You've now got to be able to write this down:

   > 48 g of Mg ......reacts to give.....80 g of MgO
   >
   > 1 g of Mg ......reacts to give.....
   >
   > 60 g of Mg ......reacts to give......

The big clue is that in the question they've said we want to burn "<u>60 g of magnesium</u>",
i.e. they've told us how much <u>magnesium</u> to have, and that's how you know to write down the
<u>left-hand side</u> of it first, because:

We'll first need to ÷ by 48 to get 1 g of Mg
and then need to × by 60 to get 60 g of Mg.

Then you can work out the numbers on the other side (shown in purple below) by realising that you must
<u>divide both sides by 48</u> and then <u>multiply both sides by 60</u>. It's tricky.

÷48 48 g of Mg .... 80 g of MgO ÷48
     1 g of Mg .... 1.67 g of MgO
×60 60 g of Mg .... 100 g of MgO ×60

The mass of product is called the <u>yield</u> of a reaction. You should realise that <u>in practice</u> you never get 100% of the yield, so the amount of product will be <u>slightly less than calculated</u> (see page 24).

This finally tells us that <u>60 g of magnesium will produce 100 g of magnesium oxide</u>.
If the question had said "Find how much magnesium gives 500 g of magnesium oxide", you'd fill in the MgO side first, <u>because that's the one you'd have the information about</u>. Got it? Good-O!

Reaction mass calculations — no worries, matey...

The only way to get good at these is to practise. So have a go at these: Answers on page 94.
1) Find the mass of calcium which gives 30 g of calcium oxide (CaO) when burnt in air.
2) What mass of fluorine (F_2) fully reacts with potassium to make 116 g of potassium fluoride (KF)?

Percentage Yield and Reversible Reactions

Percentage yield tells you about the overall success of an experiment. It compares what you calculate you should get (predicted yield) with what you get in practice (actual yield).

Percentage Yield Compares Actual and Predicted Yield

The amount of product you get is known as the yield. The more reactants you start with, the higher the actual yield will be — that's pretty obvious. But the percentage yield doesn't depend on the amount of reactants you started with — it's a percentage.

1) The predicted yield of a reaction can be calculated from the balanced reaction equation (see page 22).
2) Percentage yield is given by the formula:

$$\text{percentage yield} = \frac{\text{actual yield (grams)}}{\text{predicted yield (grams)}} \times 100$$

(The predicted yield is sometimes called the theoretical yield.)

3) Percentage yield is always somewhere between 0 and 100%.
4) A 100% percentage yield means that you got all the product you expected to get.
5) A 0% yield means that no reactants were converted into product, i.e. no product at all was made.

> **Example:**
> The expected yield of the reaction of 54 g of magnesium with oxygen is 90 g of MgO. The actual yield was 88 g of MgO. Calculate the percentage yield of this reaction.
>
> Percentage yield = (88 / 90) × 100 = **97.8%**

Yields Are Always Less Than 100%

Even though no atoms are gained or lost in reactions, in real life, you never get a 100% percentage yield. Some product or reactant always gets lost along the way — and that goes for big industrial processes as well as school lab experiments. There are several reasons for this:

1) The reaction is reversible:

> A **reversible reaction** is one where the **products** of the reaction can **themselves react** to produce the **original reactants**
>
> A + B ⇌ C + D
>
> **For example:**
> ammonium chloride ⇌ ammonia + hydrogen chloride

This means that the reactants will never be completely converted to products (the reaction does not go to completion) because the reaction goes both ways. Some of the products are always reacting together to change back to the original reactants. This will mean a lower yield.

2) When you filter a liquid to remove solid particles, you nearly always lose a bit of liquid or a bit of solid. So, some of the product may be lost when it's separated from the reaction mixture.

3) Things don't always go exactly to plan. Sometimes there can be other unexpected reactions happening which use up the reactants.
This means there's not as much reactant to make the product you want.

You can't always get what you want...

A high percentage yield means there's not much waste reactant — which is good for preserving resources, and keeping production costs down. If a reaction's going to be worth doing commercially, it generally has to have a high percentage yield or recyclable reactants. Learn the formula for working out all important percentage yield.

Section One — Fundamental Ideas in Chemistry

Revision Summary for Section One

There wasn't anything too ghastly in this section, and a few bits were even quite interesting I reckon. But you've got to make sure the facts are all firmly embedded in your brain and that you really understand the issues. These questions will let you see what you know and what you don't. If you get stuck on any, you need to look at that stuff again. Keep going till you can do them all without coming up for air.

1) A substance keeps the same volume, but changes its shape according to the container it's in. Is it a solid, a liquid or a gas?
2) Are the forces of attraction between the particles in a liquid stronger or weaker than those in a gas?
3) Describe what happens when a substance changes from a liquid to a gas.
4) What is diffusion?
5) Describe an experiment that you can do to show particles diffusing.
6) Sketch the nuclear model of an atom.
Give three details about the nucleus and three details about the electrons.
7) Draw a table showing the relative masses and charges of the three types of particle in an atom.
8)* What are the symbols for: a) calcium, b) carbon, c) sodium?
9) How many electrons are in the outer shell of an atom of a Group 7 element?
10) Which element's properties are more similar to magnesium's: calcium or iron?
11) Define the term isotope.
12) a) Define relative atomic mass.
b)* Find A_r for: i) Ca, ii) Ag (use the periodic table at the front of the book).
13) Describe how you would work out the electronic structure of an atom, given its atomic number.
14) Write out the electronic structure of potassium.
(Use the periodic table at the front of the book to help.)
15) Describe the process of ionic bonding.
16) What is covalent bonding?
17) a) Define relative formula mass.
b)* Find M_r for these (use the periodic table at the front of the book):
i) $MgCO_3$ ii) Na_2CO_3 iii) ZnO iv) KOH v) NH_3
18) What is the link between moles and relative formula mass?
19)* How many moles are there in 147 g of sodium hydroxide (NaOH)?
20)* What is the mass of 0.05 moles of magnesium oxide (MgO)?
21)* a) Calculate the percentage mass of carbon in: i) $CaCO_3$ ii) CO_2 iii) CH_4
b) Calculate the percentage mass of metal in: i) Na_2O ii) Fe_2O_3 iii) Al_2O_3
22) a) What is an empirical formula?
b)* Find the empirical formula of the compound formed when 21.9 g of magnesium, 29.2 g of sulfur and 58.4 g of oxygen react.
23)* Balance these symbol equations:
a) $Na + H_2O \rightarrow NaOH + H_2$ b) $Al + HCl \rightarrow AlCl_3 + H_2$
24) What do the following state symbols stand for?
a) (l)   b) (aq)   c) (g)
25)* a) What mass of sodium oxide (Na_2O) is produced when 50 g of sodium is burnt in air?
b) Briony does this reaction and ends up with 42.3 g of sodium oxide. What is the percentage yield of her reaction?
26) Describe three factors that can reduce the percentage yield of a reaction.

Answers on page 94.

Section One — Fundamental Ideas in Chemistry

Section Two — Bonding and Structure

Compounds and Ionic Bonding

Bonding is what keeps the atoms in a compound joined together so it's super-important. There are different types of bonding but in <u>ionic bonding</u> atoms lose or gain electrons. Read on to learn all about it...

Compounds Are Chemically Bonded

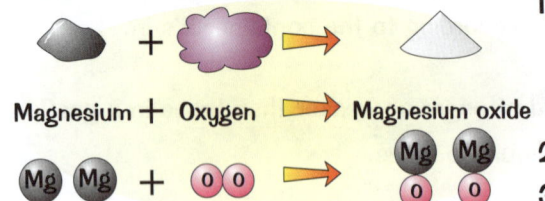

1) As you know, compounds are formed when <u>atoms</u> of <u>two or more</u> elements are <u>chemically combined</u> together. For example, magnesium oxide is a <u>compound</u> formed from a <u>chemical reaction</u> between magnesium and oxygen.
2) It's difficult to <u>separate</u> the two original elements out again.
3) The bonding that joins the atoms in a compound can be <u>ionic</u> or <u>covalent</u> — and you'll meet both in this section.

Ionic Bonding — Transferring Electrons

In <u>ionic bonding</u>, atoms <u>lose or gain outer shell electrons</u> to form <u>charged particles</u> (called <u>ions</u>) which are then <u>strongly attracted</u> to one another (because of the attraction of opposite charges, + and −).

A Shell with Just One Electron is Well Keen to Get Rid...

<u>All</u> the atoms over at the <u>left-hand side</u> of the periodic table, e.g. <u>sodium, potassium, calcium</u> etc. have just <u>one or two electrons</u> in their outer shell (highest energy level). And they're <u>pretty keen to get shot of them</u>, because then they'll only have <u>full shells</u> left, which is how they <u>like</u> it. (They try to have the same <u>electronic structure</u> as a <u>noble gas</u>.) So given half a chance they do get rid, and that leaves the atom as an <u>ion</u> instead. Now ions aren't the kind of things that sit around quietly watching the world go by. They tend to <u>leap</u> at the first passing ion with an <u>opposite charge</u> and stick to it like glue.

A Nearly Full Shell is Well Keen to Get That Extra Electron...

On the <u>other side</u> of the periodic table, the elements in <u>Group 6</u> and <u>Group 7</u>, such as <u>oxygen</u> and <u>chlorine</u>, have outer shells which are <u>nearly full</u>. They're obviously pretty keen to <u>gain</u> that <u>extra one or two electrons</u> to fill the shell up. When they do of course they become <u>ions</u> (you know, not the kind of things to sit around) and before you know it, <u>pop</u>, they've latched onto the atom (ion) that gave up the electron a moment earlier. The reaction of sodium and chlorine is a <u>classic case</u>:

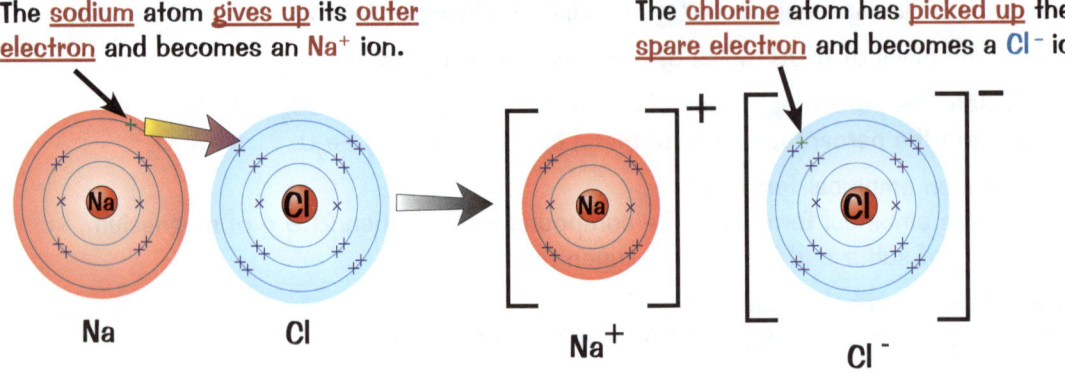

The <u>sodium</u> atom <u>gives up</u> its <u>outer electron</u> and becomes an Na^+ ion.

The <u>chlorine</u> atom has <u>picked up</u> the <u>spare electron</u> and becomes a Cl^- ion.

NaCl (Sodium Chloride)

Atoms that <u>lose electrons</u> become <u>positively charged</u> ions (e.g. the sodium atom in the reaction above).
Atoms that <u>gain electrons</u> become <u>negatively charged</u> ions (e.g. the chlorine atom in the reaction above).

Ionic dating, it's all down to chemistry — they do say opposites attract...

Ionic bonding is all about attraction between oppositely charged ions — that's what holds ionic compounds together... with maybe a little love too... Sweet. Unlike a certain ionic compound you'll find on the next page.

Ions and Ionic Compounds

Ionic Compounds Have A Regular Lattice Structure

1) Ionic compounds always have giant ionic lattices.
2) The ions form a closely packed regular lattice arrangement.
3) There are very strong electrostatic forces of attraction between oppositely charged ions, in all directions.
4) A single crystal of sodium chloride (salt) is one giant ionic lattice, which is why salt crystals tend to be cuboid in shape. The Na^+ and Cl^- ions are held together in a regular lattice.

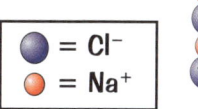
● = Cl^-
● = Na^+

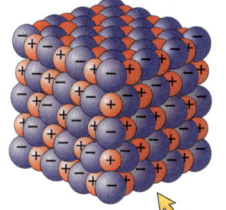

Ionic Compounds All Have Similar Properties

1) They all have high melting points and high boiling points due to the strong attraction between the oppositely charged ions. It takes a large amount of energy to overcome this attraction. When ionic compounds melt, the ions are free to move and they'll carry electric current.
2) They do dissolve easily in water though. The ions separate and are all free to move in the solution, so they'll carry electric current.

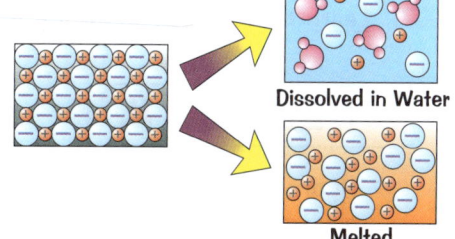
Dissolved in Water
Melted

Groups 1 & 2 and 6 & 7 are the Most Likely to Form Ions

1) Remember, atoms that have lost or gained an electron (or electrons) are ions.
2) Ions have the electronic structure of a noble gas.
3) The elements that most readily form ions are those in Groups 1, 2, 6 and 7.
4) Group 1 and 2 elements are metals and they lose electrons to form positive ions.
5) For example, Group 1 elements (the alkali metals) form ionic compounds with non-metals where the metal ion has a 1+ charge. E.g. K^+Cl^-.
6) Group 6 and 7 elements are non-metals. They gain electrons to form negative ions.
7) For example, Group 7 elements (the halogens) form ionic compounds with the alkali metals where the halide ion has a 1− charge. E.g. Na^+Cl^-.
8) The charge on the positive ions is the same as the group number of the element:

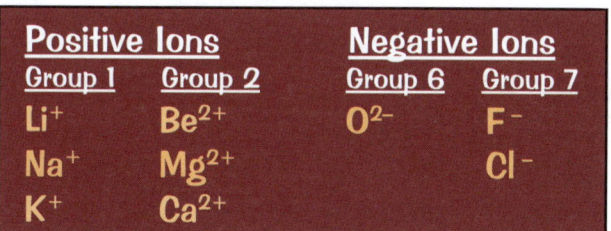

Positive Ions		Negative Ions	
Group 1	Group 2	Group 6	Group 7
Li^+	Be^{2+}	O^{2-}	F^-
Na^+	Mg^{2+}		Cl^-
K^+	Ca^{2+}		

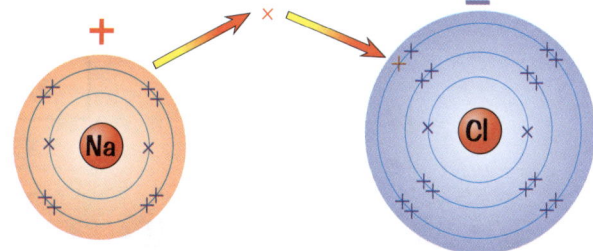

9) Any of the positive ions above can combine with any of the negative ions to form an ionic compound.
10) Only elements at opposite sides of the periodic table will form ionic compounds, e.g. Na and Cl, where one of them becomes a positive ion and one becomes a negative ion.

Remember, the + and − charges we talk about, e.g. Na^+ for sodium, just tell you what type of ion the atom WILL FORM in a chemical reaction. In sodium metal there are only neutral sodium atoms, Na. The Na^+ ions will only appear if the sodium metal reacts with something like water or chlorine.

Giant ionic lattices — all over your chips...

These guys are tough nuts to crack, but if you do crack 'em, they get all excited and start conducting electricity.

Section Two — Bonding and Structure

Covalent Bonding

Some elements bond ionically (see previous page) but others form strong covalent bonds. This is where atoms share electrons with each other so that they've got full outer shells.

Covalent Bonds — Sharing Electrons

1) Sometimes atoms prefer to make covalent bonds by sharing electrons with other atoms.
2) They only share electrons in their outer shells (highest energy levels).
3) This way both atoms feel that they have a full outer shell, and that makes them happy. Having a full outer shell gives them the electronic structure of a noble gas.
4) Each covalent bond provides one extra shared electron for each atom.
5) So, a covalent bond is a shared pair of electrons.
6) Each atom involved has to make enough covalent bonds to fill up its outer shell.
7) Learn these seven important examples:

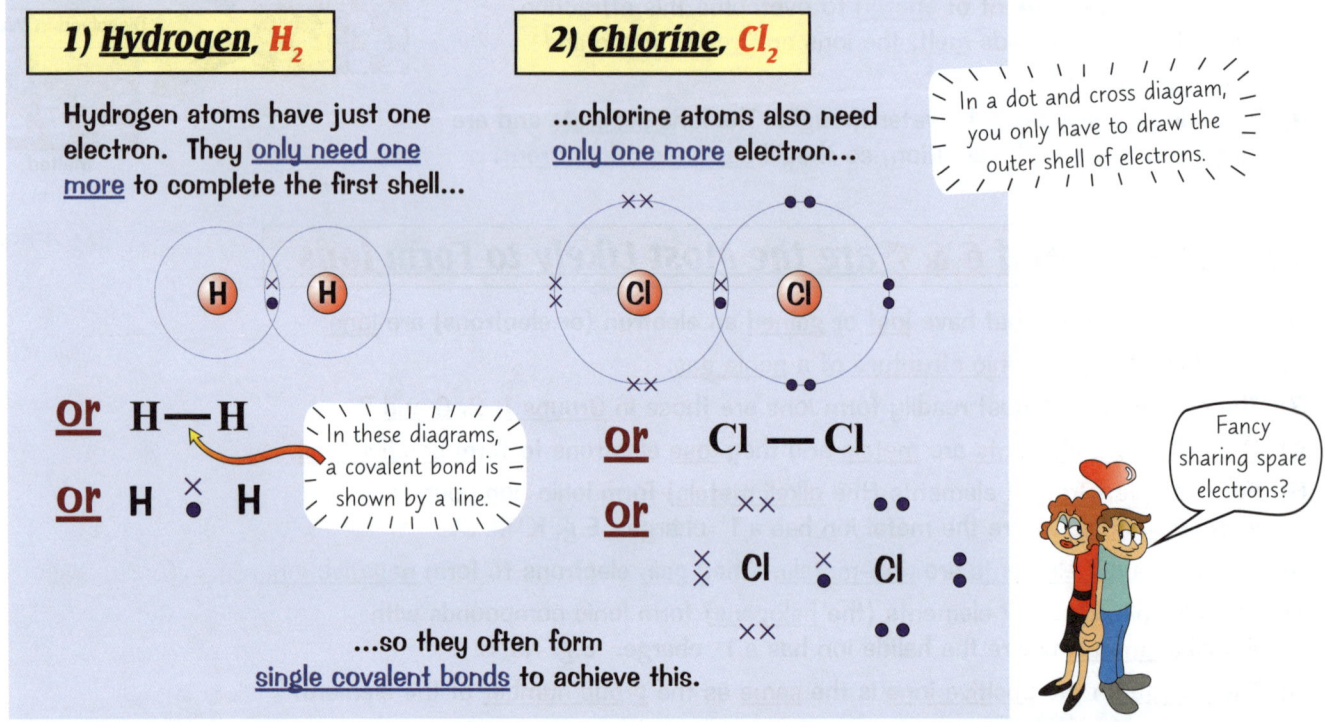

1) Hydrogen, H_2
Hydrogen atoms have just one electron. They only need one more to complete the first shell...

In these diagrams, a covalent bond is shown by a line.

2) Chlorine, Cl_2
...chlorine atoms also need only one more electron...

In a dot and cross diagram, you only have to draw the outer shell of electrons.

...so they often form single covalent bonds to achieve this.

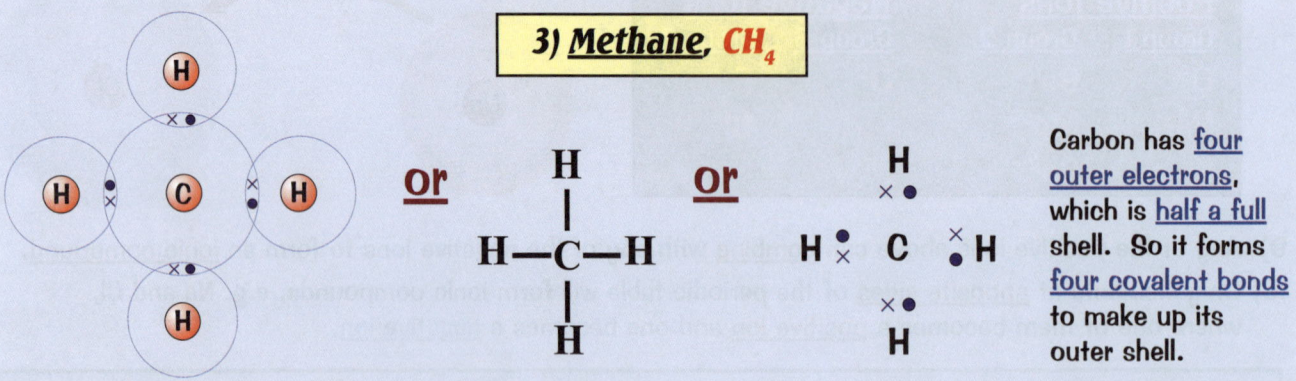

3) Methane, CH_4

Carbon has four outer electrons, which is half a full shell. So it forms four covalent bonds to make up its outer shell.

Covalent bonding — it's good to share...

There's another page of covalent bonding diagrams yet to come, but make sure you can draw the diagrams for the covalent compounds on this page first. When you've drawn a dot and cross diagram, it's a really good idea to count up the number of electrons, just to double check you've definitely got a full outer shell.

Section Two — Bonding and Structure

More Covalent Bonding

You lucky thing. There are four more examples of covalent bonding on this page — and for each compound there are three possible diagrams. I make that twelve diagrams in total... and just a smattering of words. So, this page is a breeze compared to others out there.

4) Hydrogen Chloride, HCl

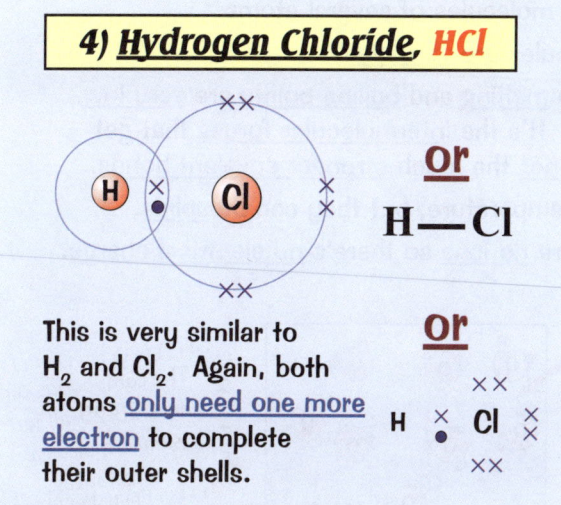

This is very similar to H_2 and Cl_2. Again, both atoms only need one more electron to complete their outer shells.

5) Ammonia, NH_3

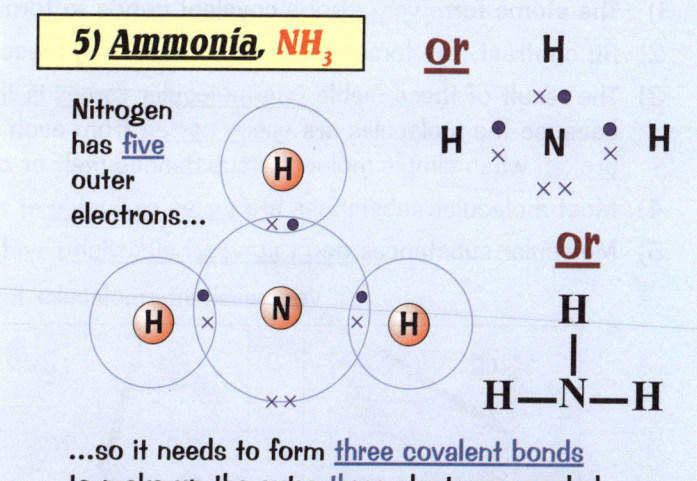

Nitrogen has five outer electrons...

...so it needs to form three covalent bonds to make up the extra three electrons needed.

6) Water, H_2O

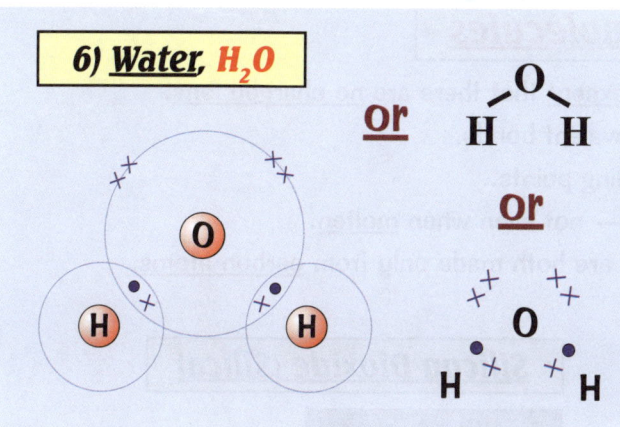

Remember — it's only the outer shells that share electrons with each other.

Oxygen atoms have six outer electrons. They sometimes form ionic bonds by taking two electrons to complete their outer shell. However they'll also cheerfully form covalent bonds and share two electrons instead. In water molecules, the oxygen shares electrons with the two H atoms.

7) Oxygen, O_2

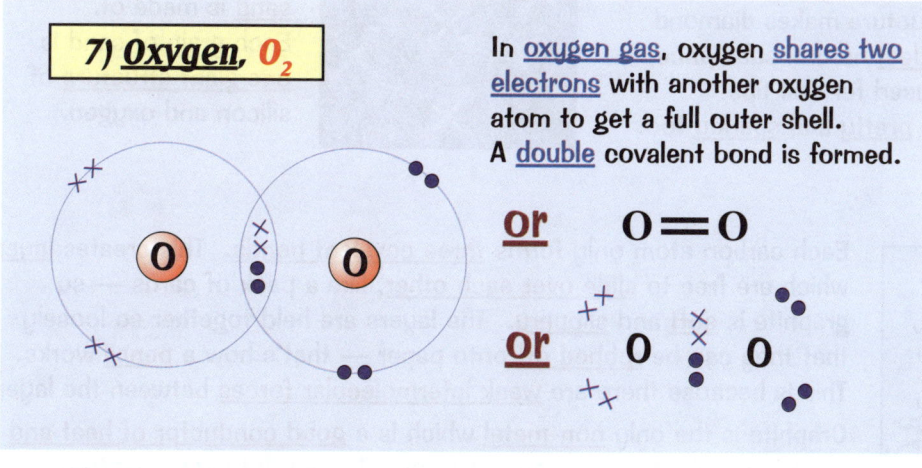

In oxygen gas, oxygen shares two electrons with another oxygen atom to get a full outer shell. A double covalent bond is formed.

The name's Bond, Covalent Bond...

Make sure you learn these seven really basic examples and why they work. Every atom wants a full outer shell, and they can get that either by becoming an ion (see page 26) or by sharing electrons. Once you understand that, you should be able to apply it to any example they give you in the exam.

Section Two — Bonding and Structure

Covalent Substances: Two Kinds

Substances with covalent bonds (electron sharing) can either be simple molecules or giant structures (macromolecules if you want the fancy word). It's non-metals that form these covalent molecules.

Simple Molecular Substances

1) The atoms form very strong covalent bonds to form small molecules of several atoms.
2) By contrast, the forces of attraction between these molecules are very weak.
3) The result of these feeble intermolecular forces is that the melting and boiling points are very low, because the molecules are easily parted from each other. It's the intermolecular forces that get broken when simple molecular substances melt or boil — not the much stronger covalent bonds.
4) Most molecular substances are gases or liquids at room temperature, but they can be solids.
5) Molecular substances don't conduct electricity — there are no ions so there's no electrical charge.

Very weak intermolecular forces

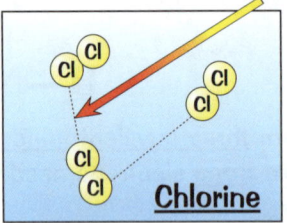
Chlorine

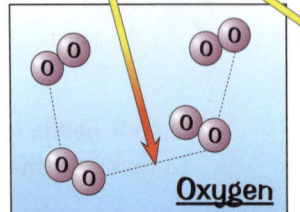
Oxygen

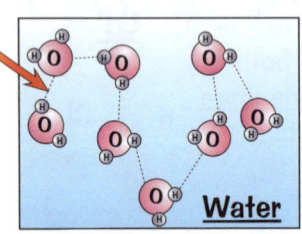
Water

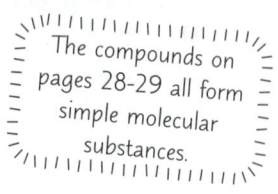
The compounds on pages 28-29 all form simple molecular substances.

Giant Covalent Structures Are Macromolecules

1) These are similar to giant ionic structures (lattices) except that there are no charged ions.
2) All the atoms are bonded to each other by strong covalent bonds.
3) This means that they have very high melting and boiling points.
4) They don't conduct electricity (except for graphite) — not even when molten.
5) The main examples are diamond and graphite, which are both made only from carbon atoms, and silicon dioxide (silica).

Diamond

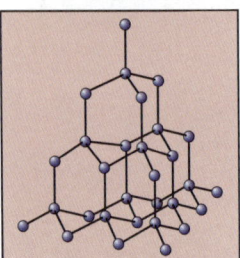

Each carbon atom forms four covalent bonds in a very rigid giant covalent structure. This structure makes diamond the hardest natural substance, so it's used for drill tips. And it's pretty and sparkly too.

Silicon Dioxide (Silica)

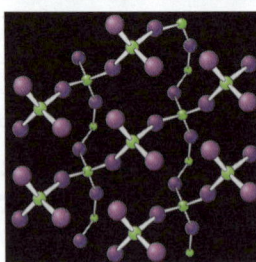

Sometimes called silica, this is what sand is made of. Each grain of sand is one giant structure of silicon and oxygen.

Graphite

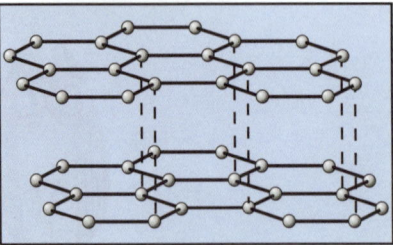

Each carbon atom only forms three covalent bonds. This creates layers which are free to slide over each other, like a pack of cards — so graphite is soft and slippery. The layers are held together so loosely that they can be rubbed off onto paper — that's how a pencil works. This is because there are weak intermolecular forces between the layers.

Graphite is the only non-metal which is a good conductor of heat and electricity. Each carbon atom has one delocalised (free) electron and it's these free electrons that conduct heat and electricity.

Carbon is a girl's best friend...

The two different types of covalent substance are very different — make sure you know about them both. You should be able to recognise a giant structure by looking at diagrams of its bonding.

Fullerenes and Nanoscience

It was an... itsy bitsy teeny weeny... teeny weeny incy wincy particle. OK, so it doesn't make for quite so 'catchy' a tune but it's what this page is all about. (Look there are even some yellow polka dotty bits...)

Nanoparticles Are Really Really Really Really Tiny ...smaller than that.

1) Really tiny particles, 1–100 nanometres across, are called 'nanoparticles' (1 nm = 0.000 000 001 m).

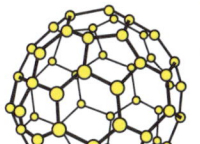

2) Nanoparticles contain roughly a few hundred atoms.
3) Nanoparticles include fullerenes. These are molecules of carbon, shaped like hollow balls or closed tubes. The carbon atoms are arranged in hexagonal rings. Different fullerenes contain different numbers of carbon atoms.
4) A nanoparticle has very different properties from the 'bulk' chemical that it's made from — e.g. fullerenes have different properties from big lumps of carbon.

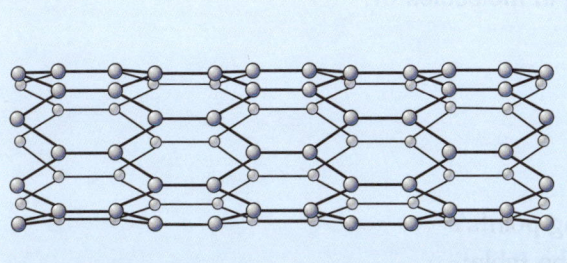

1) Fullerenes can be joined together to form nanotubes — teeny tiny hollow carbon tubes, a few nanometres across.
2) All those covalent bonds make carbon nanotubes very strong. They can be used to reinforce graphite in tennis rackets.

Nanoscience Is The Study Of Nanoparticles

Using nanoparticles is known as nanoscience. Many new uses of nanoparticles are being developed:

1) They have a huge surface area to volume ratio, so they could help make new industrial catalysts (see page 62).
2) You can use nanoparticles to make sensors to detect one type of molecule and nothing else. These highly specific sensors are already being used to test water purity.
3) Nanotubes can be used to make stronger, lighter building materials.
4) New cosmetics, e.g. sun tan cream and deodorant, have been made using nanoparticles. The small particles do their job but don't leave white marks on the skin.

5) Nanomedicine is a hot topic. The idea is that tiny fullerenes are absorbed more easily by the body than most particles. This means they could deliver drugs right into the cells where they're needed.
6) New lubricant coatings are being developed using fullerenes. These coatings reduce friction a bit like ball bearings and could be used in all sorts of places from artificial joints to gears.
7) Nanotubes conduct electricity, so they can be used in tiny electric circuits for computer chips.

Super strong tennis rackets and teeny weeny computer chips — cool...

Some nanoparticles have really unexpected properties. Silver's normally very unreactive, but silver nanoparticles can kill bacteria. Cool. On the flipside, we also need to watch out for any unexpected harmful properties. Some research has suggested that nanoparticles in medicines might accumulate in body tissues and be toxic. Not cool.

Section Two — Bonding and Structure

Revision Summary for Section Two

Some people skip these pages. But what's the point in reading a whole section if you're not going to check if you really know it or not? Look, just read the first ten questions, and I guarantee there'll be an answer you'll have to look up. And when it comes up in the exam, you'll be so glad you did.

1) What is a compound?
2) Describe the process of ionic bonding.
3)* Draw a diagram to show the electronic structure of an Mg^{2+} ion (magnesium's atomic number is 12).
4) Describe the structure of a crystal of sodium chloride.
5) List the main properties of ionic compounds.
6) What type of ion do elements from the following groups form?
   a) Group 1
   b) Group 7
7) What is covalent bonding?
8) Sketch dot and cross diagrams showing the bonding in molecules of:
   a) hydrogen,
   b) hydrogen chloride,
   c) ammonia,
   d) water
9) Give three examples of giant covalent structures.
10) Why do simple molecular substances have low boiling points?
11)* Identify the structure of each of the substances in the table:

Substance	Melting point (°C)	Electrical conductivity
A	−218.4	Zero
B	2072	Zero
C	605	Zero in solid form High when molten

12) What are nanoparticles?
13) Describe the structure of a fullerene.
14) Give two different uses of nanoparticles.

* Answers on page 94.

Section Two — Bonding and Structure

Section Three — Air and Water

Air

We take air for granted — breathing it in and out and never giving it a second thought. Surprisingly it's not just one thing, it's made up of lots of different chemicals. Oxygen is my favourite...

The Air Contains Various Chemicals

1) The Earth is surrounded by a mixture of gases — the air.
2) Air is mostly made up of nitrogen and oxygen:

   Nitrogen 78%
   Oxygen 21%

3) The figures above are rounded slightly — air also contains small amounts of argon, carbon dioxide, neon and varying amounts of water vapour.
4) Each of the different gases in air have different boiling points.

Here's a picture of the Earth from space.

The blue haze around the Earth is air.

Oxygen and Nitrogen Can Be Separated from Air

Dry air can be fractionally distilled to get a variety of products (e.g. nitrogen and oxygen) for use in industry. Carbon dioxide and water vapour must be removed first, and then fractional distillation can be used to separate oxygen and nitrogen from the rest of the air.

1) Air is filtered to remove dust.
2) It's then cooled to around -200 °C and becomes a liquid.
3) During cooling water vapour condenses and is removed.
4) Carbon dioxide freezes and is removed.
5) The liquified air then enters the fractionating column and is heated slowly.
6) The remaining gases are separated by fractional distillation. Oxygen and argon come out together so another column is used to separate them.

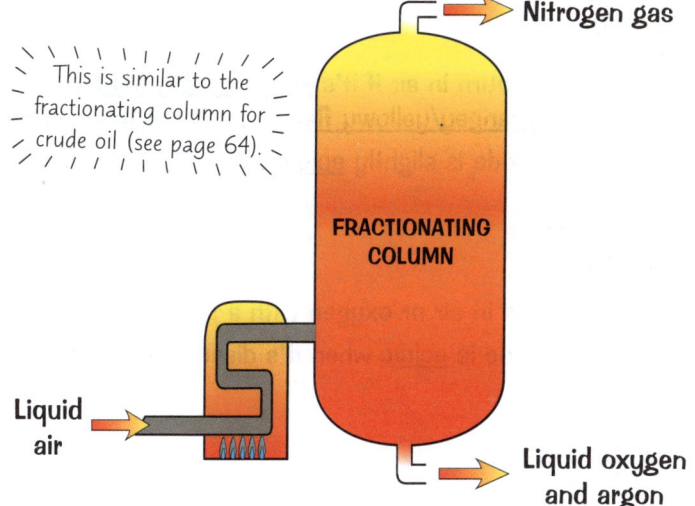

This is similar to the fractionating column for crude oil (see page 64).

Testing for Oxygen

1) You can test for oxygen using a glowing spill.
2) If you put the glowing spill into a test tube containing oxygen, it will relight.

Glowing spill

You can't see air — but it's there...

Lots of people think that air is mostly oxygen, but really it's mostly nitrogen — oxygen's only about a fifth of it. Make sure you know the other gases in air too, and how nitrogen and oxygen can be separated from it.

Oxygen and Burning

This page has lots of reactions involving oxygen. You need to learn how it reacts with other elements to form oxides — more commonly known as "what happens when you burn something".

When you Burn Something it Reacts with Oxygen in Air

1) When an element is burnt in air it reacts with the oxygen to form an oxide.
2) This is an oxidation reaction — oxygen is being added.
3) The opposite of this is a reduction reaction, where oxygen is removed.

Oxides Can Be Acidic, Basic or Amphoteric

1) Oxides are usually either acidic or basic, but they can also be amphoteric. Amphoteric means the oxide can react either as an acid or as a base.
2) If you dissolve an oxide in water, it will form an acidic or alkaline solution.
   - Metal oxides give alkaline solutions
   - Non-metal oxides give acidic solutions
3) Here are some examples of oxidation reactions that you need to know:

Magnesium

Magnesium burns with a bright white flame in air and the white powder that is formed is magnesium oxide. Magnesium oxide is slightly alkaline when it's dissolved in water.

$$2Mg_{(s)} + O_{2(g)} \rightarrow 2MgO_{(s)}$$

Carbon

Carbon will burn in air if it's very strongly heated. It has an orangey/yellowy flame and it produces carbon dioxide gas. Carbon dioxide is slightly acidic when it's dissolved in water.

$$C_{(s)} + O_{2(g)} \rightarrow CO_{2(g)}$$

Sulfur

Sulfur burns in air or oxygen with a pale blue flame and produces sulfur dioxide. Sulfur dioxide is acidic when it's dissolved in water.

$$S_{(s)} + O_{2(g)} \rightarrow SO_{2(g)}$$

Sodium

Sodium burns in air with a bright yellow flame and the white solid that's formed is sodium oxide. Sodium oxide is alkaline when it's dissolved in water.

$$4Na_{(s)} + O_{2(g)} \rightarrow 2Na_2O_{(s)}$$

Iron

Iron burns in air if it's heated very strongly. It has an orange flame and the black powder that's formed is iron oxide. Iron oxide does not dissolve in water.

$$4Fe_{(s)} + 3O_{2(g)} \rightarrow 2Fe_2O_{3(s)}$$

It's a good job they don't make park benches out of magnesium...

Quite a bit to remember here. You need to learn how oxygen reacts with magnesium, carbon, sulfur, sodium and iron. And, if that wasn't enough, you also need to know how to tell whether an oxide will give an acidic or alkaline solution when it's dissolved in water — just remember: metal oxide = alkaline, non-metal oxide = acidic.

Section Three — Air and Water

Air Pollution

You don't have to be studying for a qualification in chemistry to know that burning fuel can produce pollution. But seeing as you are studying for a qualification in chemistry you'd best learn the details. Here they are...

Burning Fuels Can Produce Pollutants

When fuels are burnt, pollutants such as carbon monoxide, nitrogen oxides and sulfur dioxide may be produced...

Carbon Monoxide is Produced by Incomplete Combustion

1) Carbon monoxide (CO) is formed when hydrocarbon fuels (e.g. petrol or diesel in car engines, or gas in central heating) are burnt without enough oxygen — this is partial combustion (see page 66).
2) Carbon monoxide is poisonous — it can stop your blood doing its proper job of carrying oxygen around the body. It combines irreversibly with haemoglobin in blood cells, meaning the blood can carry less oxygen.
3) A lack of oxygen in the blood can lead to fainting, a coma or even death.

Sulfur Dioxide and Nitrogen Oxides Come from Burning Fuel

1) Sulfur dioxide (SO_2) and nitrogen oxides are also released when fossil fuels are burnt.
2) The sulfur dioxide comes from sulfur impurities in the fossil fuels.
3) Nitrogen oxides are created when the temperature is high enough for the nitrogen and oxygen in the air to react. This often happens in car engines. Nitrogen oxides include nitrogen monoxide (NO) and nitrogen dioxide (NO_2).

Acid Rain is Caused by Sulfur Dioxide and Nitrogen Oxides

1) All rain is slightly acidic because carbon dioxide in the air reacts with water to produce a slightly acidic solution.
2) But when sulfur dioxide mixes with clouds it forms dilute sulfuric acid, which is much more acidic.
3) Nitrogen oxides can also form nitric acid in clouds.
4) The rain that falls from these clouds is called acid rain.

$$CO_{2(g)} + H_2O_{(l)} \rightarrow H_2CO_{3(aq)}$$
carbon dioxide + water → carbonic acid

$$2SO_{2(g)} + O_{2(g)} + 2H_2O_{(l)} \rightarrow 2H_2SO_{4(aq)}$$
sulfur dioxide + oxygen + water → sulfuric acid

5) Acid rain causes lakes to become acidic and many plants and animals die as a result.
6) Acid rain kills trees and damages limestone buildings and ruins stone statues. It's shocking.
7) Links between acid rain and human health problems have been suggested.

A recent survey found that most trees now fear clouds... I don't blame 'em...

So, sulfur dioxide and nitrogen oxides cause acid rain, and carbon monoxide poisoning could even kill you. Bad news all round. How about a cheese joke to cheer you up? Yes? Excellent. Here goes... Did you hear about the explosion at the French cheese factory? All that was left was de brie. Ba-boom. Ah, how we laughed...

Section Three — Air and Water

Water Quality

It's easy to take water for granted... turn on the tap, and there it is — nice, clean water. The water you drink's been round the block a few times — so there's some fancy chemistry needed to make it drinkable.

Use Cobalt Chloride Paper to Test For Water

1) If you want to test for water, you can use cobalt chloride paper. If the blue paper turns pink, it means water is present.
2) This test will tell you if water is present in a solution but it won't tell you if the water is pure.

- When a sample is pure it means it's only made up of one substance.
- This means it has set defined physical properties like boiling point and freezing point.

Pure water will always: Boil at 100 °C
Freeze at 0 °C

If you find the boiling point isn't 100 °C or freezing point isn't 0 °C then the sample isn't pure.

To Make Pure Water You Need to Remove Salts

Natural water contains dissolved salts so it isn't pure. To make pure water you need to remove the salts.

1) Totally pure water with nothing dissolved in it can be produced by distillation — boiling water to make steam and condensing the steam.
2) This process is too expensive to produce tap water — bags of energy would be needed to boil all the water we use.
3) However, in some very dry countries, e.g. Kuwait, sea water is distilled to remove the salt and produce drinking water. This is called desalination.

Drinking Water Needs to Be Good Quality

1) To be good enough for drinking, water must only have low levels of dissolved salts (e.g. nitrates) and must be free of harmful microbes. Microbes in water can cause diseases such as cholera and dysentery.
2) Most of our drinking water comes from reservoirs. Water flows into reservoirs from rivers and groundwater — water companies choose to build reservoirs where there's a good supply of clean water. Government agencies keep a close eye on pollution in reservoirs, rivers and groundwater.

Water from reservoirs goes to the water treatment works for treatment:

1) The water passes though a mesh screen to remove big bits like twigs.
2) Chemicals are added to make solids and microbes stick together and fall to the bottom.
3) The water is filtered through gravel beds to remove all the solids.
4) Water is chlorinated to kill off any harmful microbes left.

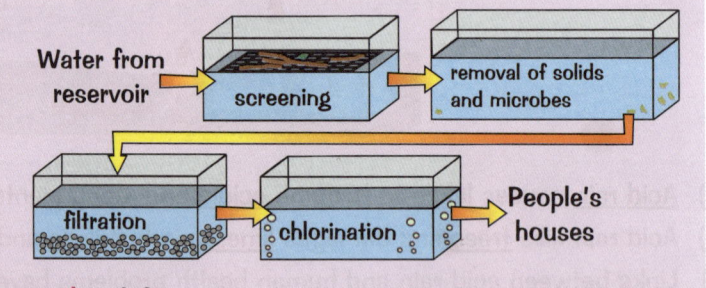

The water you drink has been through 7 people already...

Well, it's possible. It's also possible that the water you're drinking used to be part of the Atlantic Ocean. Or it could have been drunk by Alexander the Great. Or part of an Alpine glacier. Aye, it gets about a bit, does water. And remember... tap water isn't pure — but it's drinkable, and that's the main thing.

Section Three — Air and Water

Water Quality

We're not finished with water yet... there's more filtering that can be done and other chemicals to add.

Water Filters Can Improve the Taste and Quality of Water

Even after water treatment, some people still aren't satisfied. They buy filters to remove more substances from their tap water.

Carbon Water Filters

1) Some people don't like the taste of water after it has had chlorine added to kill microbes.
2) Luckily they can use a carbon water filter to remove the chlorine taste.
3) The carbon filter has a very large surface area which traps impurities, like chlorine, but lets the rest of the water flow through.

Silver Water Filters

1) Silver water filters can be used to stop bacteria and other nasty bugs growing in the water.
2) So as the water passes through the filter, you're left with clean water.

Ion Resin Exchanges

1) Hard water contains a lot of calcium and magnesium ions, which can cause problems. For example, pipes, boilers and kettles can become 'scaled-up' which reduces their efficiency.
2) So some people living in hard water areas buy water softeners, which contain ion exchange resins.

The water supply is fed through an ion exchange resin which removes the hardness. The resin contains lots of sodium ions (or hydrogen ions) and 'exchanges' them for calcium or magnesium ions in the water that runs through them.

e.g. $Na_2Resin(s) + Ca^{2+}(aq) \rightarrow CaResin(s) + 2Na^+(aq)$

A resin is a solid polymer that's insoluble in water.

Adding Fluoride and Chlorine to Water Has Disadvantages

1) Fluoride is added to drinking water in some parts of the country because it helps to reduce tooth decay.
2) Chlorine is added to kill microbes and prevent disease. So far so good. However...
3) Some studies have linked adding chlorine to water with an increase in certain cancers. Chlorine can react with other natural substances in water to produce toxic by-products which some people think could cause cancer.
4) In high doses fluoride can cause cancer and bone problems in humans, so some people believe that fluoride shouldn't be added to drinking water. There is also concern about whether it's right to 'mass medicate' — people can choose whether to use a fluoride toothpaste, but they can't choose whether their tap water has added fluoride.
5) Levels of chemicals added to drinking water need to be carefully monitored. For example, in some areas the water may already contain a lot of fluoride, so adding more could be harmful.

Put the chlorine in, take the chlorine out, in, out, in, out...

That's it for water treatment, but before you move on, make sure you really know it. Learn about the different types of filters that can be used and what they are used for. Then you'll also need to know why fluoride and chlorine are added to water and why this might not be such a good idea. Best start now then...

Section Three — Air and Water

Rust

Iron's strength has made it a very important metal that's used throughout the world for building construction, car manufacture and wrought iron garden furniture. But the problem is — it rusts...

Iron Corrodes to Make Rust

1) Iron corrodes easily. In other words, it rusts. The word "rust" is only used for the corrosion of iron, not other metals.
2) The chemical reaction that takes place when iron corrodes is an oxidation reaction. The iron gains oxygen to form iron(III) oxide.
3) Water then becomes loosely bonded to the iron(III) oxide and the result is hydrated iron(III) oxide — which we call rust.
4) Here's the word equation for the reaction:

> iron + oxygen + water → hydrated iron(III) oxide (rust)

5) Unfortunately, rust is a soft crumbly solid that soon flakes off to leave more iron available to rust again.

Both Air and Water are Needed for Iron to Rust

1) Rusting only happens when iron is in contact with both oxygen (from the air) and water.
2) If you put an iron nail in a boiling tube with just water, it won't rust. (The water is boiled to remove oxygen and oil is used to stop air getting in.)
3) If you put an iron nail in a boiling tube with just air, it won't rust. (Calcium chloride can be used to absorb any water from the air.)

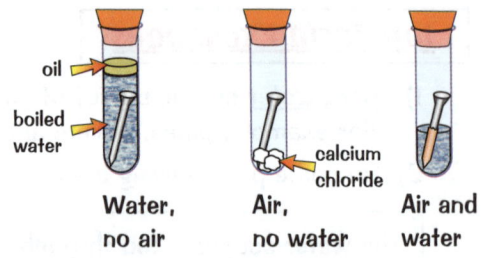

Water, no air | Air, no water | Air and water

There are Two Main Ways to Prevent Rusting

1) The obvious way to prevent rusting is to coat the iron with a barrier to keep out the water and oxygen.

   BARRIER METHODS:
   - Painting/Coating with plastic — ideal for big and small structures alike. It can be decorative too.
   - Oiling/Greasing — this has to be used when moving parts are involved, like on bike chains.

2) The other way is the sacrificial method. This involves placing a more reactive metal with the iron. The water and oxygen then react with this sacrificial metal instead of with the iron.

   - Zinc is often used as a sacrificial metal.
   - The zinc is more reactive than iron — it's further up the reactivity series.
   - So, the zinc will be oxidised instead of the iron.
   - A coating of zinc can be sprayed onto the object — this is known as galvanising.
   - Or big blocks of zinc can be bolted to the iron. This is used on ships' hulls, or on underground iron pipes.

Jamie wanted to make sure his Nan didn't rust.

The sacrificial method — who knew chemistry could sound so bloodthirsty...

So there you have it folks. If you've wondered how Iron Man avoids rusting, it's a combination of greasing himself up and sending out Zinc Man if it's raining. Make sure you learn all the stuff on this page by covering the page and writing it all out again — not that you need me to remind you of the method of course...

Section Three — Air and Water

Revision Summary for Section Three

Air and water — pretty important things. The one thing that's constant and unchanging is the need to learn it all for the exam you've got coming up. So test yourself on these little beauties.

1) Name the two main gases that make up the air.
2) In what proportion are the main gases in the air found?
3) What other gases are found in the air?
4) Why do we fractionally distill air?
5) What is the test for oxygen gas?
6) What type of reaction occurs when you burn something in air?
7) What happens in a reduction reaction?
8) Describe the reaction of oxygen with magnesium.
9) When non-metal oxides dissolve in water, do they form acidic solutions or alkaline solutions?
10) Describe the reaction of oxygen with carbon.
11) What conditions are needed for the production of carbon monoxide when a fuel is burnt?
12) Why is carbon monoxide poisonous?
13) How is sulfur dioxide formed?
14) Explain how nitrogen oxides are formed from burning fuels. Where is this likely to happen?
15) Why are nitrogen oxides and sulfur dioxide bad for the environment?
16) What test can you do to see whether water is present?
17) How can you tell if a sample of water is pure?
18) Explain why tap water isn't usually purified by distillation.
19) What is the role of the gravel beds in water treatment?
20) During water treatment, how are microbes killed so that the water is safe to drink?
21) Why is fluoride added to some drinking water?
22) Give one disadvantage of adding fluoride to drinking water.
23) Which metal rusts?
24) Describe an experiment you could carry out to show that both air and water are needed for rust to form.
25) Describe two ways that rusting can be prevented.

Section Three — Air and Water

Section Four — The Periodic Table and Metals

More About The Periodic Table

Glance back at page 16 if you're confused by the 'More' in the title. This nice table appeared there too.

The Periodic Table is Based on Atomic Number

1) The elements in the periodic table are arranged in order of increasing atomic (proton) number.
2) They're also arranged so that elements with similar properties are in columns called groups. The table is called a 'periodic' table because similar properties appear at regular intervals — or periods.

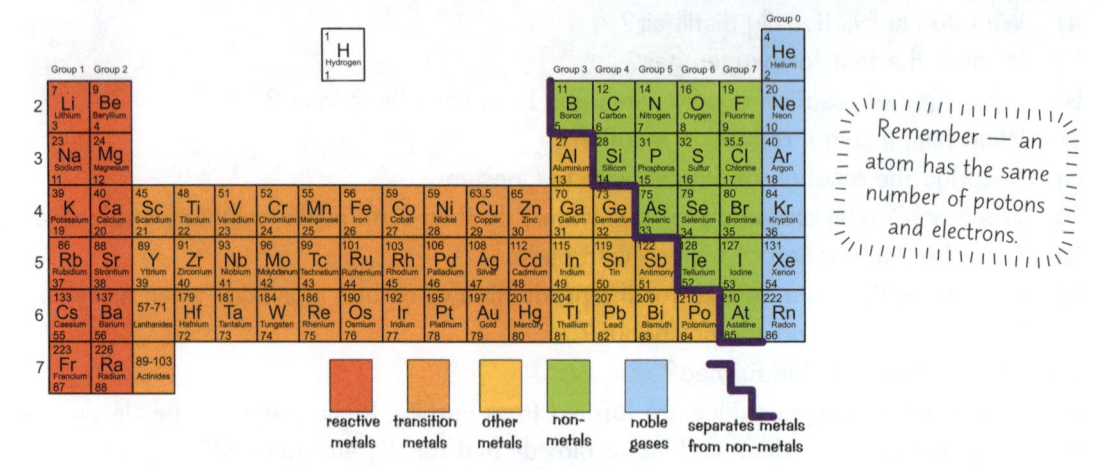

Remember — an atom has the same number of protons and electrons.

reactive metals | transition metals | other metals | non-metals | noble gases | separates metals from non-metals

3) Electrons in an atom are set out in shells which each correspond to an energy level.
4) Apart from the transition metals, elements in the same group in the periodic table have the same number of electrons in their outer shell (highest occupied energy level) — this is what gives them similar properties. So if you know an element's electronic structure, you can predict its chemical properties.
5) The group number is equal to the number of electrons in the highest occupied energy level — e.g. Group 6 all have 6 electrons in the highest energy level.
6) The positive charge of the nucleus attracts electrons and holds them in place. The further from the nucleus the electron is, the less the attraction.
7) The attraction of the nucleus is even less when there are a lot of inner electrons. Inner electrons "get in the way" of the nuclear charge, reducing the attraction. This effect is known as shielding.
8) The combination of increased distance and increased shielding means that an electron in a higher energy level is more easily lost because there's less attraction from the nucleus holding it in place. That's why Group 1 metals get more reactive as you go down the group.
9) Increased distance and shielding also means that a higher energy level is less likely to gain an electron — there's less attraction from the nucleus pulling electrons into the atom. That's why Group 7 elements get less reactive going down the group.

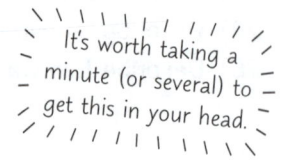

It's worth taking a minute (or several) to get this in your head.

Group 0 Elements are All Inert, Colourless Gases

1) Group 0 elements are called the noble gases and include the elements helium, neon and argon (plus a few others).
2) They are inert — this means they don't react with much at all.
3) The reason for this is that they have a stable arrangement of electrons — they all have a full outer shell. (A full outer shell is 8 electrons for all the noble gases except helium, which has 2.) This means they're not desperate to give up or gain electrons.

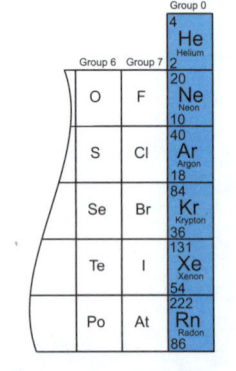

Group 0 elements are inert — wherever Ert is...

In the exam, you could be asked questions like "Use electronic structure to explain why caesium is more reactive than sodium". If you've learnt this page you'll know that it's to do with it being further down the group...

Group 1 — The Alkali Metals

The alkali metals are silvery solids that have to be stored in oil and handled with forceps (they burn the skin).

Learn These Trends:

As you go DOWN Group 1, the alkali metals:
1) become MORE REACTIVE
   ...because the outer electron is more easily lost, because it's further from the nucleus.
2) have LOWER MELTING AND BOILING POINTS

The alkali metals have LOW DENSITY. In fact, the first three in the group are less dense than water.

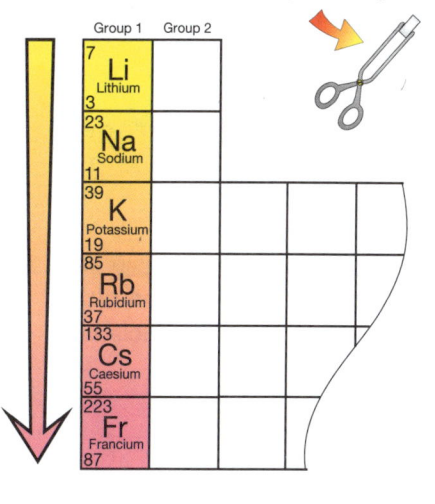

1) They are: Lithium, Sodium, Potassium and a Couple More

Know those three names real well. They may also mention rubidium and caesium.

2) The Alkali Metals All Have ONE Outer Electron

This makes them very reactive and gives them all similar properties.

3) The Alkali Metals Form Ionic Compounds with Non-Metals

1) They are keen to lose their one outer electron to form a 1+ ion.
2) They are so keen to lose the outer electron there's no way they'd consider sharing, so covalent bonding is out of the question.
3) So they always form ionic bonds — and they produce white compounds that dissolve in water to form colourless solutions.

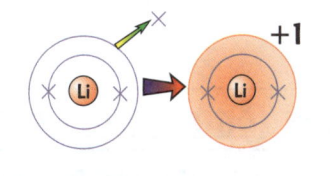

4) Reaction with Water Produces Hydrogen Gas

1) When lithium, sodium or potassium are put in water, they react very vigorously.
2) They float and move around the surface, fizzing furiously.
3) They produce hydrogen. Potassium gets hot enough to ignite it. A lighted spill will indicate hydrogen by producing the notorious "squeaky pop" as the H_2 ignites (see page 44).
4) They form hydroxides that dissolve in water to give alkaline solutions.

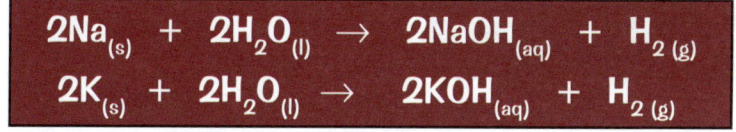

$$2Na_{(s)} + 2H_2O_{(l)} \rightarrow 2NaOH_{(aq)} + H_{2(g)}$$
$$2K_{(s)} + 2H_2O_{(l)} \rightarrow 2KOH_{(aq)} + H_{2(g)}$$

The solution becomes alkaline (hence the name alkali metals), which changes the colour of universal indicator to purple.

2 trends and 4 properties — not much to learn at all...

I'm no gambler, but I'd put money on a question like this in the exam: "Using your knowledge of the Group 1 metals, describe what would happen if a piece of caesium were put into water." Just use what you know about the other Group 1 metals... you're going to get H_2, and a pretty violent reaction.

Section Four — The Periodic Table and Metals

Group 7 — The Halogens

The 'trend thing' happens in Group 7 as well — that shouldn't come as a surprise.
But some of the trends are kind of the opposite of the Group 1 trends. Remember that.

Learn These Trends:

As you go DOWN Group 7, the HALOGENS have the following properties:

1) **LESS REACTIVE**
   ...because it's harder to gain an extra electron, because the outer shell's further from the nucleus.
2) **HIGHER MELTING POINT**
3) **HIGHER BOILING POINT**

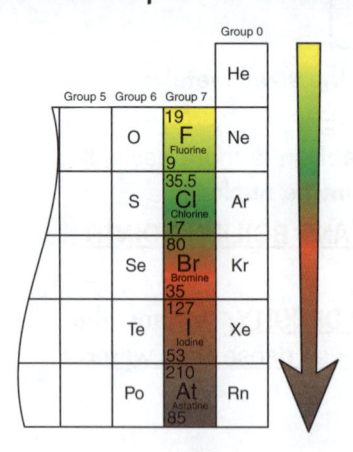

1) The Halogens are All Non-metals with Coloured Vapours

Fluorine is a very reactive, poisonous yellow gas.
Chlorine is a fairly reactive, poisonous dense green gas.
Bromine is a dense, poisonous, red-brown volatile liquid.
Iodine is a dark grey crystalline solid or a purple vapour.

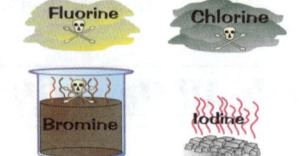

They all exist as molecules which are pairs of atoms:

F_2 Cl_2 Br_2 I_2

2) The Halogens Form Ionic Bonds with Metals

The halogens form 1^- ions called halides (F^-, Cl^-, Br^- and I^-) when they bond with metals, for example Na^+Cl^-.
The diagram shows the bonding in sodium chloride, NaCl.

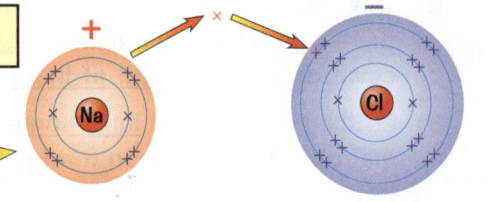

3) More Reactive Halogens Will Displace Less Reactive Ones

A more reactive halogen can displace (kick out) a less reactive halogen from an aqueous solution of its salt.
E.g. chlorine can displace bromine and iodine from an aqueous solution of its salt (a bromide or iodide).
Bromine will also displace iodine because of the trend in reactivity.

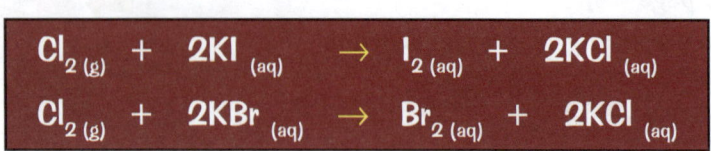

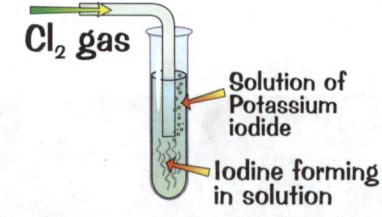

$$Cl_{2\,(g)} + 2KI_{(aq)} \rightarrow I_{2\,(aq)} + 2KCl_{(aq)}$$

$$Cl_{2\,(g)} + 2KBr_{(aq)} \rightarrow Br_{2\,(aq)} + 2KCl_{(aq)}$$

Polish that halo and get revising...

Once more, you don't have to be a mind-reader to be able to guess the kind of thing they're going to ask you in the exam. My money's on something to do with displacement reactions — will iodine displace bromine from some compound or other, for instance. Learn the facts... just learn the facts.

Section Four — The Periodic Table and Metals

Transition Elements

Transition elements make up the big clump of metals in the middle of the periodic table.

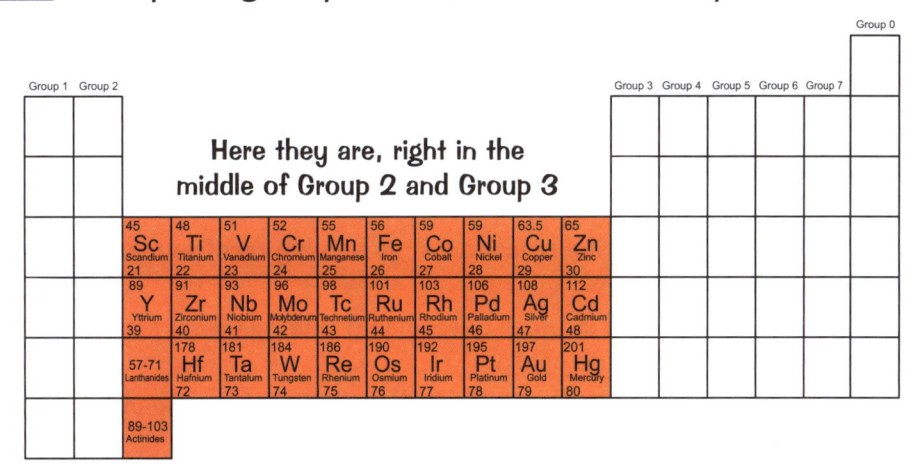

Here they are, right in the middle of Group 2 and Group 3

Transition elements (or transition metals) are typical metals, and have the properties you would expect of a 'proper' metal:

1) They're good conductors of heat and electricity.
2) They're very dense, strong and shiny.
3) Transition metals are much less reactive than Group 1 metals — they don't react as vigorously with water or oxygen, for example.
4) They're also much denser, stronger and harder than the Group 1 metals, and have much higher melting points (except for mercury, which is a liquid at room temperature). E.g. iron melts at 1500 °C, copper at 1100 °C and zinc at 400 °C.

Transition Metals Often Have More Than One Ion, e.g. Fe^{2+}, Fe^{3+}

Two other examples are copper: Cu^+ and Cu^{2+} and chromium: Cr^{2+} and Cr^{3+}.
The different ions usually form different-coloured compounds too:
Fe^{2+} ions usually give green compounds, whereas Fe^{3+} ions usually form red/brown compounds (e.g. rust).

The Compounds are Very Colourful

1) The compounds are colourful due to the transition metal ion they contain, e.g. Potassium chromate(VI) is yellow. Potassium manganate(VII) is purple. Copper(II) sulfate is blue.
2) The colours in gemstones, like blue sapphires and green emeralds, and the colours in pottery glazes are all due to transition metals. And weathered copper is a lovely colourful green.

Transition Metals and Their Compounds All Make Good Catalysts

1) Iron is the catalyst used in the Haber process (see page 82) for making ammonia.
2) Manganese(IV) oxide is a good catalyst for the decomposition of hydrogen peroxide.
3) Nickel is useful for turning oils into fats for making margarine.

Catalysts increase the rate of a reaction — see page 62.

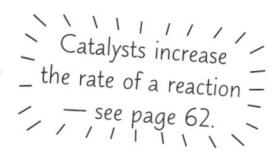

Shiny metals, pretty colours, catalysts — we've got it all...

Most common everyday metals are transition elements — for example, iron, nickel, copper, silver, gold... You need to know that transition metals form ions with different charges, form coloured compounds and make good catalysts — oh, and you need to be able to compare them with the Group 1 metals.

Section Four — The Periodic Table and Metals

Reactions of Metals

Different metals react differently with water or dilute acids, depending on their reactivity.

Metals React with Dilute Acids to Produce Salts

Acid + Metal → Salt + Hydrogen

Here's the typical experiment:
1) The more reactive the metal, the faster the reaction will go — very reactive metals (e.g. sodium) react explosively.
2) This means that metals can be arranged in order of reactivity (the reactivity series — see next page) from their reactions with dilute acids.
3) The speed of reaction is indicated by the rate at which the bubbles of hydrogen are given off.
4) The hydrogen is confirmed by the burning spill test. Hydrogen makes a "squeaky pop" with a lighted spill. (The noise comes from the hydrogen burning with the oxygen in the air to form H_2O.)
5) Potassium, sodium and lithium all react very violently with dilute acids.
6) Copper doesn't react with dilute acids.

Here are some more examples:

CALCIUM — Calcium reacts violently with cold dilute acids and produces loads of bubbles.

MAGNESIUM — Magnesium reacts vigorously with cold dilute acids and produces a lot of bubbles.

ZINC and **IRON** — Both zinc and iron react slowly with dilute acids but more strongly if you heat them up.

Metals Also React with Water

The reactions of metals with water also show the reactivity of metals.

Metal + Water → Metal Hydroxide + Hydrogen
(Less reactive Metal + Steam → Metal oxide + Hydrogen)

1) Very reactive metals like potassium, sodium, lithium and calcium will all react vigorously with water.
2) Less reactive metals like magnesium, zinc and iron won't react much with cold water but they will react with steam.
3) Copper won't react with either water or steam.

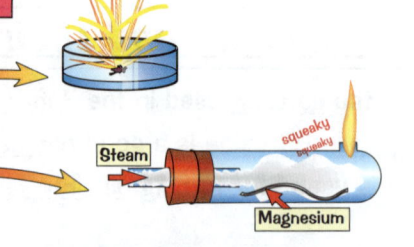

Bubbles bubbles bubbles bubbles — I love the bubbles...

There's enough on this page to make the revision juices bubble more than a lump of potassium in a tube of dilute acid. If you react metals with water or dilute acid you'll get this order of reactivity from most reactive to least reactive: Potassium, Sodium, Lithium, Calcium, Magnesium, Zinc, Iron, Copper.

Section Four — The Periodic Table and Metals

The Reactivity Series

If you have two different metals, you can use a displacement reaction to find out which one is most reactive. If you do this lots of times with lots of different metals, you can put the metals in order of their reactivity.

A More Reactive Metal Displaces a Less Reactive Metal

1) Metal compounds like copper sulfate, zinc chloride and sodium chloride are metal salts. If you put a reactive metal into an aqueous solution of a less reactive metal salt the reactive metal will replace the less reactive metal in the salt.

An aqueous solution of something just means it's dissolved in water.

> Example: put a strip of magnesium in an aqueous solution of copper sulfate and the more reactive magnesium will "kick out" the less reactive copper from the salt. You end up with magnesium sulfate solution and copper metal:
>
> copper sulfate + magnesium → magnesium sulfate + copper
> $CuSO_{4(aq)} + Mg_{(s)} \rightarrow MgSO_{4(aq)} + Cu_{(s)}$

2) You can describe displacement reactions in terms of oxidation (loss of electrons) and reduction (gain of electrons). This means you can also write an ionic equation:

> In the reaction between copper sulfate and magnesium, the magnesium atom (Mg) loses two electrons (is oxidised) to become a magnesium ion (Mg^{2+}). The copper ion (Cu^{2+}) gains two electrons (is reduced) to become a copper atom (Cu).
>
> copper ion + magnesium → magnesium ion + copper
> $Cu^{2+}_{(aq)} + Mg_{(s)} \rightarrow Mg^{2+}_{(aq)} + Cu_{(s)}$ ← This is an ionic equation

The sulfate ion (SO_4^{2-}) doesn't change, so it's not in the ionic equation.

3) If you put a piece of silver metal into an aqueous solution of copper sulfate instead, nothing happens. This is because the more reactive metal (copper) is already in the salt.

4) You can use displacement reactions to work out where in the reactivity series a metal is supposed to go.

The Reactivity Series — How Well a Metal Reacts

1) The reactivity series lists metals in order of their reactivity towards other substances.

2) The non-metals carbon and hydrogen are sometimes included in this list for comparison.

3) Metal oxides below carbon can be reduced by heating with carbon (there's more on this on the next page). Metals below hydrogen won't react with dilute acids.

Make sure you learn this list:

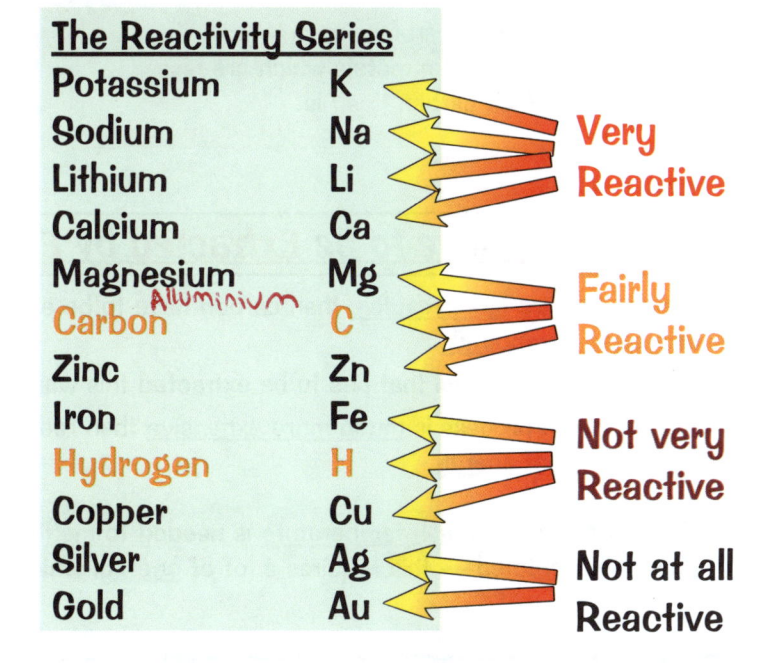

The Reactivity Series

Potassium	K	Very Reactive
Sodium	Na	
Lithium	Li	
Calcium	Ca	
Magnesium	Mg	
Carbon (Alluminium)	C	Fairly Reactive
Zinc	Zn	
Iron	Fe	Not very Reactive
Hydrogen	H	
Copper	Cu	
Silver	Ag	Not at all Reactive
Gold	Au	

I AM NOT HIGHLY REACTIVE — OK...

What is the world coming to. Metals fighting it out to get their filthy paws on some measly salts. "Why do we care about their petty squabbles?", I hear you cry. Well, dear reader, just turn the page and you'll find out...

Section Four — The Periodic Table and Metals

Getting Metals From Rocks

It's time to find out how all that reactivity stuff (page 45) is useful in real life. Well, as you know, we use lots of stuff made of metal. But most metals aren't sitting around as pure lumps waiting to be made into fighter jets, drawing pins and chocolate fountain machines (seriously?) — they have to be extracted.

Most Metals are Found in Ores

1) Metals that are unreactive don't tend to form compounds with other elements. Unreactive metals such as gold are found uncombined — so you just have to find them and dig 'em up.
2) However, most metals do react with other elements to form compounds, which can be found naturally in the Earth's crust. If a compound contains enough of the metal to make it worthwhile extracting, the compound is called a metal ore. There are limited amounts of metal ores — they're "finite resources".
3) The more reactive a metal is, the harder it is to extract it from a compound.

Some Metals can be Extracted by Reduction with Carbon

1) Most metal ores are oxides. A metal can be extracted from its ore chemically by reduction using carbon.
2) When an ore is reduced, oxygen is removed from it, e.g.

$$2Fe_2O_3 + 3C \rightarrow 4Fe + 3CO_2$$
iron(III) oxide + carbon → iron + carbon dioxide

This is how iron is extracted in a blast furnace.

3) The position of the metal in the reactivity series determines whether it can be extracted by reduction with carbon.

a) Metals higher than carbon in the reactivity series have to be extracted using electrolysis (see below), which is expensive.

b) Metals below carbon in the reactivity series can be extracted by reduction using carbon. For example, iron oxide is reduced in a blast furnace to make iron.

This is because carbon can only take the oxygen away from metals which are less reactive than carbon itself is.

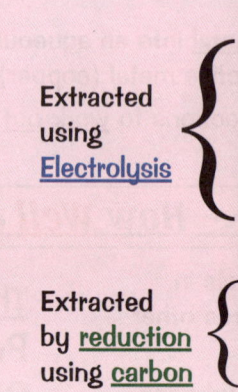

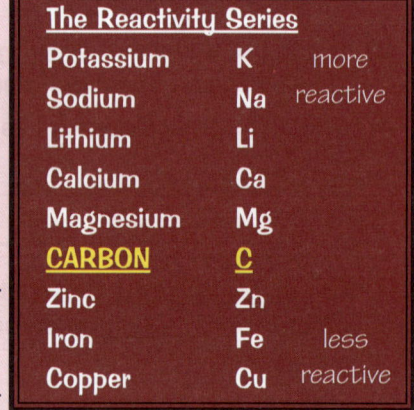

The Reactivity Series		
Potassium	K	more reactive
Sodium	Na	
Lithium	Li	
Calcium	Ca	
Magnesium	Mg	
CARBON	**C**	
Zinc	Zn	
Iron	Fe	less reactive
Copper	Cu	

Extracted using Electrolysis (Potassium through Magnesium)
Extracted by reduction using carbon (Zinc through Copper)

Some Metals have to be Extracted by Electrolysis

1) Metals that are more reactive than carbon have to be extracted using electrolysis of molten compounds.
2) An example of a metal that has to be extracted this way is aluminium (see page 86).
3) However, the process is much more expensive than reduction with carbon because it uses a lot of energy.

> FOR EXAMPLE: a high temperature is needed to melt aluminium oxide so that aluminium can be extracted — this requires a lot of energy, which makes it an expensive process.

Learn how metals are extracted — ore else...

Extracting metals isn't cheap. You have to pay for special equipment, energy and labour. Then there's the cost of getting the ore to the extraction plant. If there's a choice of extraction methods, a company always picks the cheapest, unless there's a good reason not to (e.g. to increase purity). They're not extracting it for fun.

Section Four — The Periodic Table and Metals

Getting Metals From Rocks

You may think you know all you could ever want to know about how to get metals from rocks, but no — there's more of it. Think of each of the facts on this page as a little gold nugget. Or, er, a copper one.

Copper is Purified by Electrolysis

1) Copper can easily be extracted by reduction with carbon (see previous page). The ore is heated in a furnace — this is called smelting.
2) However, the copper produced this way is impure — and impure copper doesn't conduct electricity very well. This isn't very useful because a lot of copper is used to make electrical wiring.
3) So electrolysis is also used to purify it, even though it's quite expensive.
4) This produces very pure copper, which is a much better conductor.

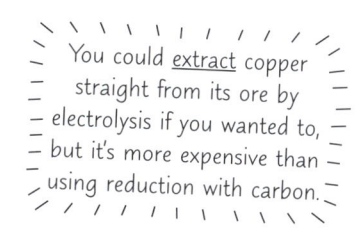

You could extract copper straight from its ore by electrolysis if you wanted to, but it's more expensive than using reduction with carbon.

Electrolysis Means "Splitting Up with Electricity"

1) Electrolysis is the breaking down of a substance using electricity.
2) It requires a liquid to conduct the electricity, called the electrolyte.
3) Electrolytes are often metal salt solutions made from the ore (e.g. copper sulfate) or molten metal oxides.
4) The electrolyte has free ions — these conduct the electricity and allow the whole thing to work.
5) Here's how electrolysis is used to get pure copper:

Cathode (−ve) — The cathode starts as a thin piece of pure copper and more pure copper adds to it.

Anode (+ve) — The electrolyte is copper(II) sulfate solution containing $Cu^{2+}(aq)$ ions. The anode is just a big lump of impure copper, which will dissolve. Sludge.

The electrical supply acts by:
- Pulling electrons off copper atoms at the anode, causing them to go into solution as Cu^{2+} ions.
- Then offering electrons at the cathode to nearby Cu^{2+} ions to turn them back into copper atoms.
- The impurities are dropped at the anode as a sludge, whilst pure copper atoms bond to the cathode.

Pure copper is deposited on the cathode (−ve)

The reaction at the cathode is:

$$Cu^{2+}(aq) + 2e^- \rightarrow Cu(s)$$

The copper ions have been reduced to copper atoms by gaining electrons.

Copper dissolves from the impure anode (+ve)

The reaction at the anode is:

$$Cu(s) \rightarrow Cu^{2+}(aq) + 2e^-$$

Copper atoms have been oxidised into copper ions by losing electrons.

These are ionic half equations.

This is a copper-bottomed cert for the exam...

The skin of the Statue of Liberty is made of copper — about 80 tonnes of it in fact. Its surface reacts with the gases in the air to form copper carbonate — which is why it's that pretty shade of green.

Section Four — The Periodic Table and Metals

Getting Metals From Rocks

Just to top it off, you need to know even more about copper extraction... sigh, it's a hard life.

You Can Extract Copper From a Solution Using a Displacement Reaction

1) You saw on page 45 how more reactive metals displace less reactive metals from solutions. Well, you can use this process to extract copper from solutions of copper salts.

2) For example, scrap iron can be used to displace copper from solution — this is really useful because iron is cheap but copper is expensive.

3) If some iron is put in a solution of copper sulfate, the more reactive iron will "kick out" the less reactive copper from the solution. You end up with iron sulfate solution and copper metal:

$$\text{copper sulfate} + \text{iron} \rightarrow \text{iron sulfate} + \text{copper}$$
$$Cu^{2+}_{(aq)} + Fe_{(s)} \rightarrow Fe^{2+}_{(aq)} + Cu_{(s)}$$

It's another one of those ionic equations — methinks they're quite important so make sure you know how to write one.

4) In this reaction, copper is reduced (gains electrons) and iron is oxidised (loses electrons).

Copper-rich Ores are in Short Supply

1) The supply of copper-rich ores is limited, so it's important to recycle as much copper as possible.
2) The demand for copper is growing and this may lead to shortages in the future.
3) Scientists are looking into new ways of extracting copper from low-grade ores (ores that only contain small amounts of copper) or from the waste that is currently produced when copper is extracted.
4) Examples of new methods to extract copper are bioleaching and phytomining:

Bioleaching
This uses bacteria to separate copper from copper sulfide. The bacteria get energy from the bond between copper and sulfur, separating out the copper from the ore in the process. The leachate (the solution produced by the process) contains copper, which can be extracted, e.g. by filtering.

Phytomining
This involves growing plants in soil that contains copper. The plants can't use or get rid of the copper so it gradually builds up in the leaves. The plants can be harvested, dried and burned in a furnace. The copper can be collected from the ash left in the furnace.

5) Traditional methods of copper mining are pretty damaging to the environment (see next page). These new methods of extraction have a much smaller impact, but the disadvantage is that they're slow.

Personally, I'd rather be pound rich than copper rich...

Pure copper is expensive but exceptionally useful stuff. Just think where we'd be without good quality copper wire to conduct electricity (hmmm... how would I live without my electric pineapple corer). The fact that copper-rich ore supplies are dwindling means that scientists have to come up with ever-more-cunning methods to extract it. It also means that you have to learn all about it. Sorry about that.

Section Four — The Periodic Table and Metals

Impacts of Extracting Metals

Metals are very useful. Just imagine if all knives and forks were made of plastic instead — there'd be prongs snapping all over the place at dinner time. However, metal extraction uses a lot of energy and is bad for the environment. And that's where recycling comes in handy.

Metal Extraction can be Bad for the Environment

1) People have to balance the social, economic and environmental effects of mining ores such as copper ore.
2) As with most things in life, mining has both advantages and disadvantages:

> Mining metal ores is good because it means that useful products can be made. It also provides local people with jobs and brings money into the area. This means services such as transport and health can be improved.

> But mining ores is bad for the environment as it causes noise, scarring of the landscape and loss of habitats. Deep mine shafts can also be dangerous for a long time after the mine has been abandoned.

Recycling Metals is Important

1) Mining and extracting metals takes lots of energy, most of which comes from burning fossil fuels.

2) Fossil fuels are running out so it's important to conserve them. Not only this, but burning them contributes to acid rain, global dimming and climate change (see pages 66-67).

3) Recycling metals only uses a small fraction of the energy needed to mine and extract new metal. E.g. recycling copper only takes 15% of the energy that's needed to mine and extract new copper.

4) Energy doesn't come cheap, so recycling saves money too.

5) Also, there's a finite amount of each metal in the Earth. Recycling conserves these resources.

6) Recycling metal cuts down on the amount of rubbish that gets sent to landfill. Landfill takes up space and pollutes the surroundings. If all the aluminium cans in the UK were recycled, there'd be 14 million fewer dustbins to empty each year.

Get back on your bike again — recycle...

Recycling metals saves natural resources and money and reduces environmental problems. It's great. There's no limit to the number of times metals like aluminium, copper and steel can be recycled. So your humble little drink can may one day form part of a powerful robot who takes over the galaxy.

Metals

Ever wondered what makes metals tick? Well, either way, this is the page for you.

Metal Properties Are All Due to the Sea of Free Electrons

1) Metals consist of giant structures of atoms in a regular pattern.

2) Metallic bonds involve the all-important 'free electrons' which produce all the properties of metals. These delocalised (free) electrons come from the outer shell of every metal atom in the structure.

3) These electrons are free to move through the whole structure. These free moving electrons mean that metals are good conductors of heat and electricity.

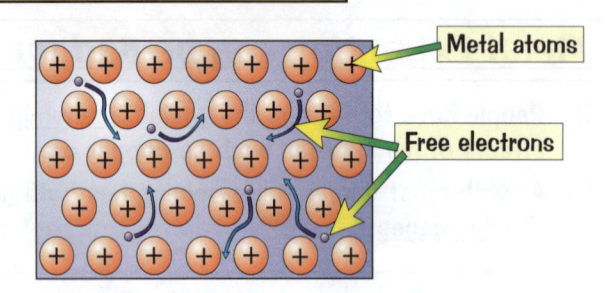

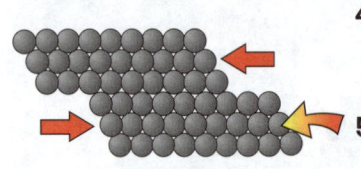

4) These electrons also hold the atoms together in a regular structure. There are strong forces of electrostatic attraction between the positive metal ions and the negative electrons.

5) They also allow the layers of atoms to slide over each other, allowing metals to be bent and shaped.

Metals are Strong and Bendy and They're Great Conductors

1) All metals have some fairly similar basic properties:
   - Metals are strong (hard to break), but they can be bent or hammered into different shapes.
   - They're great at conducting heat.
   - They conduct electricity well.

2) Metals (and especially transition metals, which are found in the centre block of the periodic table) have loads of everyday uses because of these properties...

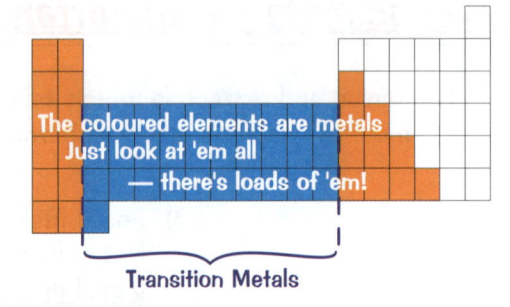

The coloured elements are metals. Just look at 'em all — there's loads of 'em!

Transition Metals

Copper is Useful for Electrical Wiring and Plumbing

1) Copper is a good conductor of electricity, so it's ideal for making electrical wires.

2) Copper is also great for use in plumbing. This is because it's below hydrogen in the reactivity series, so it doesn't react with water. Also, it can be bent, but is still hard enough to be used for pipes or tanks.

Pure Iron Tends to be a Bit Too Bendy

1) 'Iron' straight from the blast furnace is only 96% iron. The other 4% is impurities such as carbon.

2) This impure iron is used as cast iron, which is very strong when it's being compressed. Cast iron is handy for making ornamental railings, but it doesn't have many other uses because it's brittle.

3) Pure iron is far too bendy for most uses. Most iron is used to make steel — which is harder, stronger and less bendy than pure iron.

Metal fatigue? — yeah, I've had enough of this page too...

So, all metals conduct electricity and heat and can be bent into shape. But lots of them have special properties too. You have to decide what properties you need and use the metal with those properties.

Section Four — The Periodic Table and Metals

Alloys

If a metal's not quite up to the job, you can mix it with another one (or a non-metal), to get an alloy that is.

Most Iron is Converted into Steel — an Alloy

Most of the pure iron is changed into alloys called steels. Steels are formed by adding small amounts of carbon and sometimes other metals to the iron. They can be made to have specific properties:

TYPE OF STEEL	PROPERTIES	USES
Low carbon steel (0.1% carbon)	easily shaped	car bodies
High carbon steel (1.5% carbon)	very hard, inflexible	blades for cutting tools, bridges
Stainless steel (chromium added, and sometimes nickel)	corrosion-resistant	cutlery, containers for corrosive substances

Alloys are Harder Than Pure Metals

1) Alloys are usually made from two or more metals. Different elements have different sized atoms. So when an element such as carbon is added to pure iron, the smaller carbon atom will upset the layers of pure iron atoms, making it more difficult for them to slide over each other. This makes alloys harder than pure metals.

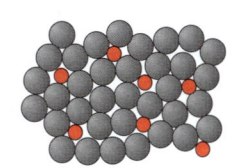

2) Most metals in everyday use are actually alloys. Pure copper, gold, iron and aluminium are too soft for most uses, so are mixed with small amounts of other metals to make them harder — and so more useful. For example:

BRONZE = COPPER + TIN Bronze is harder than copper. It's good for making medals and statues from.

GOLD ALLOYS ARE USED TO MAKE JEWELLERY Pure gold is too soft. Metals such as zinc, copper, silver, palladium and nickel are used to harden the "gold".

ALUMINIUM ALLOYS ARE USED TO MAKE AIRCRAFT Aluminium has a low density, but it's alloyed with small amounts of other metals to make it stronger.

Some Alloys Have Really Weird Properties

1) New materials are continually being developed, with new properties. Smart materials behave differently depending on the conditions, e.g. temperature.

2) A good example is nitinol — a "shape memory alloy". It's a metal alloy (about half nickel, half titanium) but when it's cool you can bend it and twist it like rubber. Bend it too far, though, and it stays bent. But here's the really clever bit — if you heat it above a certain temperature, it goes back to a "remembered" shape.

3) Nitinol is used for dental braces. In the mouth it warms and tries to return to a 'remembered' shape, and so it gently pulls the teeth with it. It's also handy for glasses frames. If you accidentally bend them, you can just pop them into a bowl of hot water and they'll jump back into shape.

A brass band — harder than Iron Maiden...

The Eiffel Tower is made of iron — but the problem with iron is, it goes rusty if air and water get to it. So the Eiffel Tower has to be painted every seven years to make sure that it doesn't rust. This is quite a job and takes an entire year for a team of 25 painters. Too bad they didn't use stainless steel.

Section Four — The Periodic Table and Metals

Revision Summary for Section Four

Well, you'll have enjoyed that if you're a metalhead. Everyone else — you can breathe a sigh of relief now. Oh no, wait — not quite yet. Test how many facts reacted with your brain and displaced some song lyrics with these lovingly hand-crafted questions. I don't make them for anyone else, you know.

1) How are elements arranged in the periodic table?
2) How are the group number and the number of electrons in the outer shell related?
3) What is shielding?
4) What are Group 0 elements called?
5) As you go down Group I, what's the trend in reactivity?
6) Describe the density of the alkali metals.
7) Write down the balanced symbol equation for the reaction between sodium and water.
8) Explain why Group 7 elements get less reactive as you go down the group from fluorine to iodine.
9) What is the charge on a halide ion when it forms an ionic compound?
10) Write down the balanced equation for the displacement of bromine from potassium bromide by chlorine.
11) Will the following reactions occur: a) iodine with lithium chloride, b) chlorine with lithium bromide?
12) Describe the physical properties of a typical transition metal.
13) What is the test for hydrogen gas?
14) Put these metals in order from most reactive to least reactive when added to dilute acid: zinc, calcium, iron, and magnesium.
15) Give the name of:
    a) a very reactive metal,
    b) a not at all reactive metal.
16) What happens when a piece of calcium is put into an aqueous solution of zinc sulfate?
17) How do most metals naturally occur?
18) Explain why zinc can be extracted by reduction with carbon but magnesium can't.
19) Give a reason why aluminium is an expensive metal.
20) What is electrolysis?
21) Describe the process of purifying copper by electrolysis.
22) Describe how scrap iron is used to displace copper from solution.
23) What is the name of the method where plants are used to extract metals from soil?
24) Give three reasons why it's good to recycle metal.
25) Give three properties of metals.
26) What is the problem with using a) iron straight from the blast furnace, b) very pure iron?
27) Why are alloys harder than pure metals?
28) Give an example of a shape memory alloy and describe how it behaves.

Section Four — The Periodic Table and Metals

Section Five — Acids, Bases and Reaction Rates

Acids and Bases

Testing the pH of a solution means using an indicator — and that means pretty colours...

The pH Scale Goes From 0 to 14

1) The pH scale is a measure of how acidic or alkaline a solution is.
2) The strongest acid has pH 0. The strongest alkali has pH 14.
3) A neutral substance has pH 7 (e.g. pure water).

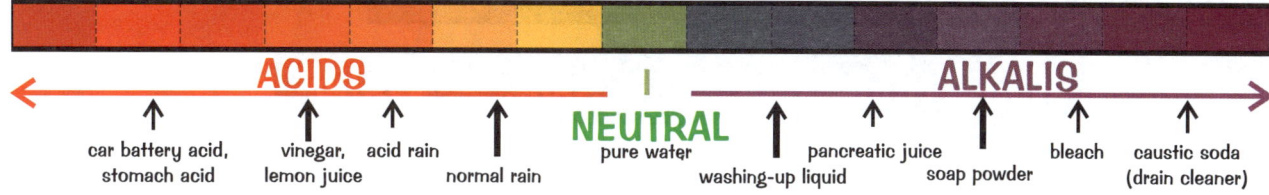

pH 0 1 2 3 4 5 6 7 8 9 10 11 12 13 14

← ACIDS | ALKALIS →

NEUTRAL

- car battery acid, stomach acid
- vinegar, lemon juice
- acid rain
- normal rain
- pure water
- washing-up liquid
- pancreatic juice
- soap powder
- bleach
- caustic soda (drain cleaner)

An Indicator is Just a Dye That Changes Colour

The dye in the indicator changes colour depending on whether it's above or below a certain pH. Indicators are very useful for estimating the pH of a solution. There are several different types:

1) Universal indicator is a very useful combination of dyes which gives the colours shown above.
2) Litmus paper tests whether a solution is acidic or alkaline because it changes colour at about pH 7. It's red in acidic solutions, purple in neutral solutions and blue in alkaline solutions. 
3) Phenolphthalein will change from colourless in acidic solutions to bright pink in alkaline solutions.
4) Methyl orange changes from red in acidic solutions to yellow in alkaline solutions.

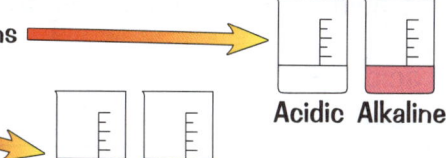

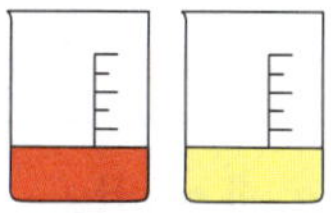

Acids and Bases Neutralise Each Other

An **ACID** is a substance with a pH of less than 7. Acids form H⁺ ions in water.
A **BASE** is a substance with a pH of greater than 7.
An **ALKALI** is a base that dissolves in water. Alkalis form OH⁻ ions in water.
So, H⁺ ions make solutions acidic and OH⁻ ions make them alkaline.

The reaction between acids and bases is called neutralisation. Make sure you learn it:

$$acid + base \rightarrow salt + water$$

Neutralisation can also be seen in terms of H⁺ and OH⁻ ions like this, so learn it too:

$$H^+_{(aq)} + OH^-_{(aq)} \rightarrow H_2O_{(l)}$$

Hydrogen (H⁺) ions react with hydroxide (OH⁻) ions to produce water.

When an acid neutralises a base (or vice versa), the products are neutral, i.e. they have a pH of 7. An indicator can be used to show that a neutralisation reaction is over (universal indicator will go green).

Interesting(ish) fact — your skin is slightly acidic (pH 5.5)...

The neutralisation reaction's a great one to know. If you have indigestion, it's because you've got too much hydrochloric acid in your stomach. Indigestion tablets contain bases that neutralise some of the acid.

Oxides, Hydroxides and Ammonia

I'm afraid there's more stuff on neutralisation reactions coming up...

Metal Oxides and Metal Hydroxides Are Bases

1) Some metal oxides and metal hydroxides dissolve in water. These soluble compounds are alkalis.
2) Even bases that won't dissolve in water will still react with acids.
3) So, all metal oxides and metal hydroxides react with acids to form a salt and water.

$$\text{Acid} + \text{Metal Oxide} \rightarrow \text{Salt} + \text{Water}$$

$$\text{Acid} + \text{Metal Hydroxide} \rightarrow \text{Salt} + \text{Water}$$

(These are neutralisation reactions of course)

The Combination of Metal and Acid Decides the Salt

This isn't exactly exciting but it's pretty easy, so try and get the hang of it:

hydrochloric acid + copper oxide	$\rightarrow$	copper chloride + water
hydrochloric acid + sodium hydroxide	$\rightarrow$	sodium chloride + water
sulfuric acid + zinc oxide	$\rightarrow$	zinc sulfate + water
sulfuric acid + calcium hydroxide	$\rightarrow$	calcium sulfate + water
nitric acid + magnesium oxide	$\rightarrow$	magnesium nitrate + water
nitric acid + potassium hydroxide	$\rightarrow$	potassium nitrate + water

The symbol equations are all pretty much the same. Here are two of them:

$$H_2SO_{4\,(aq)} + ZnO_{(s)} \rightarrow ZnSO_{4\,(aq)} + H_2O_{(l)}$$

$$HNO_{3\,(aq)} + KOH_{(aq)} \rightarrow KNO_{3\,(aq)} + H_2O_{(l)}$$

Ammonia Can be Used to Produce Ammonium Salts

Ammonia dissolves in water to make an alkaline solution: $H_2O_{(l)} + NH_{3\,(l)} \rightarrow NH_4^+{}_{(aq)} + OH^-{}_{(aq)}$
If this solution reacts with an acid, you get a salt, e.g:

$$NH_{3\,(aq)} + HNO_{3\,(aq)} \rightarrow NH_4NO_{3\,(aq)}$$
$$\text{Ammonia} + \text{Nitric acid} \rightarrow \text{Ammonium nitrate}$$

This is a bit different from most neutralisation reactions because there's NO WATER produced — just the ammonium salt.

Ammonium salts are especially good fertilisers because they contain nitrogen. Plants need nitrogen to make proteins.

There's nowt wrong wi' just spreadin' muck on it...

Not the most thrilling of pages, I'm afraid. Just loads of reactions for you to learn. Try doing different combinations of acids and alkalis. Balance them. Cover the page and scribble all the equations down. If you make any mistakes... learn it again, cover it up again, and scribble it all down again.

Section Five — Acids, Bases and Reaction Rates

Titrations

There's a nice little experiment you can do to find out how much alkali you need to neutralise an acid. As I'm feeling generous, there's also some useful stuff about concentration thrown in on this page too — you never know when it might come in handy... Probably in the exam though.

Concentration is a Measure of How Crowded Things Are

1) The concentration of a solution can be measured in moles per dm³ (i.e. moles per litre).
2) So 1 mole of stuff in 1 dm³ of solution has a concentration of 1 mole per dm³ (or 1 mol/dm³).

Remember, one mole of a substance is equal to its relative formula mass in grams — see page 20.

The more solute you dissolve in a given volume, the more crowded the solute molecules are and the more concentrated the solution.

1 litre = 1000 cm³ = 1 dm³

3) Concentration can also be measured in grams per dm³. So 56 grams of stuff dissolved in 1 dm³ of solution has a concentration of 56 grams per dm³.

Titrations are Used to Find Out Concentrations

Titrations allow you to find out exactly how much acid is needed to neutralise a quantity of alkali (or vice versa). Here's how you do a titration...

1) Using a pipette and pipette filler, add some alkali (usually 25 cm³) to a conical flask. (The pipette filler stops you getting a mouthful of alkali.)
2) Add two or three drops of indicator — phenolphthalein or methyl orange. You don't use universal indicator as it changes colour gradually — and you want a definite colour change.
3) Fill a burette with the acid. Make sure you do this BELOW EYE LEVEL — you don't want to be looking up if some acid spills over.
4) Using the burette, add the acid to the alkali a bit at a time — giving the conical flask a regular swirl. Go especially slowly (a drop at a time) when you think the end-point (colour change) is about to be reached.
5) The indicator changes colour when all the alkali has been neutralised, e.g. phenolphthalein is pink in alkalis, but colourless in acids, and methyl orange is yellow in alkalis but red in acids.
6) Record the volume of acid used to neutralise the alkali. It's best to repeat this process a few times, making sure you get (pretty much) the same answer each time — this makes for more reliable results.
7) You can then take the mean of your results.

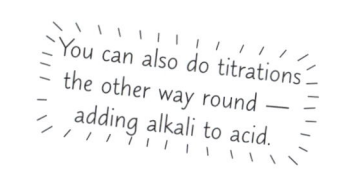

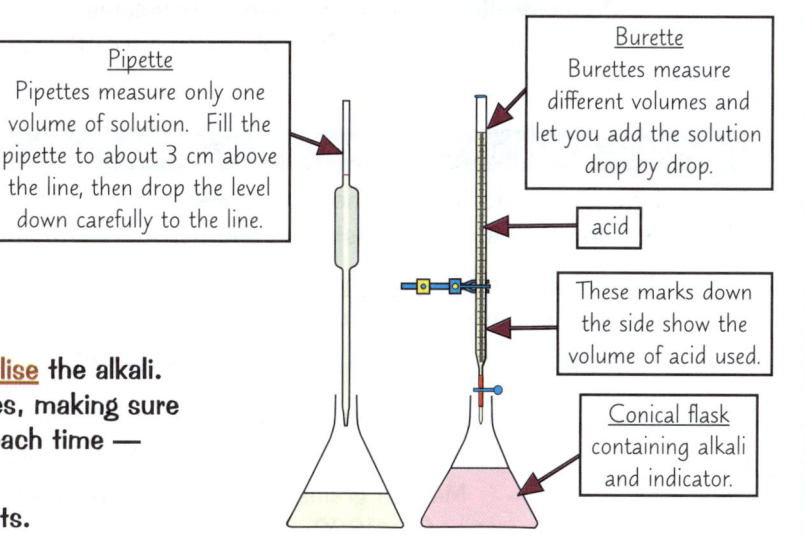

You can also do titrations the other way round — adding alkali to acid.

Prudence does everything below eye level

Pipette
Pipettes measure only one volume of solution. Fill the pipette to about 3 cm above the line, then drop the level down carefully to the line.

Burette
Burettes measure different volumes and let you add the solution drop by drop.

acid

These marks down the side show the volume of acid used.

Conical flask containing alkali and indicator.

If you can spell phenolphthalein, you deserve an A*...

There's a little bit at the end of the titration method that's pretty vital when you do any experiment — the bit about repeating the process to check your results. It's all to do with making sure your results are reliable. If you get the same result a number of times, you can have more faith in it than if it's a one-off.

Section Five — Acids, Bases and Reaction Rates

Titration Calculations

I expect you're wondering what you can do with the results from a titration experiment (who wouldn't be). Well, you'll be relieved to know that they can be used to calculate concentrations of acids or alkalis.

You Might Be Asked to Calculate the Concentration

In the exam you might be given the results of a titration experiment and asked to calculate the concentration of the acid when you know the concentration of the alkali (or vice versa).

Example 1: If they ask for concentration in MOLES per dm³

Say you start off with 25 cm³ of sodium hydroxide in your flask, and you know that its concentration is 0.1 moles per dm³.

You then find from your titration that it takes 30 cm³ of sulfuric acid (whose concentration you don't know) to neutralise the sodium hydroxide.

You can work out the concentration of the acid in moles per dm³.

Concentration = moles ÷ volume, so you can make a handy formula triangle.

Triangle: $\frac{n}{c \times V}$ — Concentration (in mol/dm³), Number of moles, Volume (in dm³). One dm³ is a litre.

Cover up the thing you're trying to find — then what's left is the formula you need to use.

Step 1: Work out how many moles of the "known" substance you have using this formula:

Number of moles = concentration × volume
= 0.1 mol/dm³ × (25 / 1000) dm³ = **0.0025 moles of NaOH**

Remember: 1000 cm³ = 1 dm³

Use the formula triangle if it helps.

Step 2: Write down the balanced equation of the reaction...

$$2NaOH + H_2SO_4 \longrightarrow Na_2SO_4 + 2H_2O$$

...and work out how many moles of the "unknown" stuff you must have had.

Using the equation, you can see that for every two moles of sodium hydroxide you had...
...there was just one mole of sulfuric acid.
So if you had 0.0025 moles of sodium hydroxide...
...you must have had 0.0025 ÷ 2 = **0.00125 moles of sulfuric acid**.

Step 3: Work out the concentration of the "unknown" stuff.

Concentration = number of moles ÷ volume
= 0.00125 mol ÷ (30 / 1000) dm³ = 0.041666... mol/dm³
= **0.0417 mol/dm³**

Don't forget to put the units.

Example 2: If they ask for concentration in GRAMS per dm³

They might ask you to find out the acid concentration in grams per cubic decimetre (grams per litre). If they do, don't panic — you just need another formula triangle.

Step 1: Work out the relative formula mass for the acid (you should be given the relative atomic masses, e.g. H = 1, S = 32, O = 16):

So, H_2SO_4 = (1 × 2) + 32 + (16 × 4) = 98

Step 2: Convert the concentration in moles (that you've already worked out) into concentration in grams. So, in 1 dm³:

Mass in grams = moles × relative formula mass
= 0.041666... × 98 = 4.08333... g

So the **concentration in g/dm³ = 4.08 g/dm³**

Use non-rounded answers in workings.

Number of moles = mass ÷ relative formula mass.

Triangle: $\frac{m}{n \times M_r}$ — Number of moles, Mass (in grams), Relative formula mass.

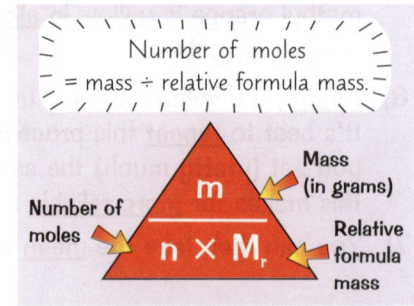

Need practice, you do — mmmm...

Scary. But if you get enough practice at these questions, then the fear will evaporate and you can tackle them with a smile on your face and a spring in your step. Remember, don't be baffled by dm³ — it's just an overly complicated way of saying "litre", that's all. So "moles per dm³" means "moles per litre". Simple.

Section Five — Acids, Bases and Reaction Rates

Making Salts

If you're making a salt it's important to know if it's soluble or not so you know which method to use. Most chlorides, sulfates and nitrates are soluble in water (the main exceptions are lead chloride, lead sulfate and silver chloride). Most oxides and hydroxides are insoluble in water.

Making Soluble Salts Using a Metal or an Insoluble Base

1) You need to pick the right acid, plus a metal or an insoluble base (a metal oxide or metal hydroxide). E.g. if you want to make copper chloride, mix hydrochloric acid and copper oxide.

   E.g. $CuO_{(s)} + 2HCl_{(aq)} \longrightarrow CuCl_{2(aq)} + H_2O_{(l)}$

2) Remember not all metals are suitable — some metals are not reactive enough and some are too reactive, e.g. copper doesn't react with dilute acids at all but sodium reacts explosively.

3) You add the metal, metal oxide or hydroxide to the acid — the solid will dissolve in the acid as it reacts. You will know when all the acid has been neutralised because the excess solid will just sink to the bottom of the flask.

4) Then filter out the excess metal, metal oxide or metal hydroxide to get the salt solution. To get pure, solid crystals of the salt, evaporate some of the water (to make the solution more concentrated) and then leave the rest to evaporate very slowly. This is called crystallisation.

Making Soluble Salts Using an Alkali

1) You can't use the method above with alkalis (soluble bases) like sodium, potassium or ammonium hydroxides, because you can't tell whether the reaction has finished — you can't just add an excess to the acid and filter out what's left.

2) You have to add exactly the right amount of alkali to just neutralise the acid — you need to use an indicator (see page 53) to show when the reaction's finished. Then repeat using exactly the same volumes of alkali and acid so the salt isn't contaminated with indicator.

3) Then just evaporate off the water to crystallise the salt as normal.

Making Insoluble Salts — Precipitation Reactions

1) If the salt you want to make is insoluble, you can use a precipitation reaction.

2) You just need to pick two solutions that contain the ions you need. E.g. to make lead chloride you need a solution which contains lead ions and one which contains chloride ions. So you can mix lead nitrate solution (most nitrates are soluble) with sodium chloride solution (all group 1 compounds are soluble).

3) Once the salt has precipitated out (and is lying at the bottom of your flask), all you have to do is filter it from the solution, wash it and then dry it on filter paper.

   E.g. $Pb(NO_3)_{2(aq)} + 2NaCl_{(aq)} \longrightarrow PbCl_{2(s)} + 2NaNO_{3(aq)}$

4) Precipitation reactions can be used to remove poisonous ions (e.g. lead) from drinking water. Calcium and magnesium ions can also be removed from water this way — they make water "hard", which stops soap lathering properly. Another use of precipitation is in treating effluent (sewage) — again, unwanted ions can be removed.

Get two beakers, mix 'em together — job's a good'n...

In the exam, you could be asked to describe how to make a given soluble or insoluble salt. You need to think carefully about what chemicals you'd need to get the salt you want and what method you'd use.

Section Five — Acids, Bases and Reaction Rates

Metal Carbonates and Limestone

Limestone's often formed from sea shells, so you might not expect that it'd be useful as a building material...

Limestone is Mainly Calcium Carbonate

Limestone is mainly calcium carbonate — $CaCO_3$, and is quarried out of the ground.

It has lots of different uses:

1) It's great for making into blocks for building with. Fine old buildings like cathedrals are often made purely from limestone blocks.
2) Calcium carbonate is an alkali so powdered limestone is used to neutralise acidic soil on fields.
3) It's used in the manufacture of cement, glass and iron.
4) It is also heated to produce lime (calcium oxide), which can be used as a building material.

St Paul's Cathedral is made from limestone.

Metal Carbonates React with Acids

Even though limestone is pretty sturdy stuff, don't go thinking it doesn't react with anything. It reacts with acid in the same way as other metal carbonates. The general reaction is:

> Acid + Metal Carbonate → Salt + Water + Carbon Dioxide

The reaction is the same as any other neutralisation reaction EXCEPT that carbonates give off carbon dioxide as well.

Thermal Decomposition of Metal Carbonates

1) When limestone is heated it thermally decomposes to make calcium oxide and carbon dioxide.

> calcium carbonate → calcium oxide + carbon dioxide
> $CaCO_{3(s)}$ → $CaO_{(s)}$ + $CO_{2(g)}$

Thermal decomposition is when one substance chemically changes into at least two new substances when it's heated.

2) When magnesium, copper, zinc and lithium carbonates are heated, they decompose in the same way. E.g. magnesium carbonate → magnesium oxide + carbon dioxide (i.e. $MgCO_3$ → $MgO + CO_2$)
3) However, you might have difficulty doing some of these reactions in class — a Bunsen burner can't reach a high enough temperature to thermally decompose some carbonates of Group I metals.

Limewater is Used as a Test for Carbon Dioxide

1) When you add water to calcium oxide you get calcium hydroxide.

> calcium oxide + water ⟶ calcium hydroxide   or $CaO + H_2O \longrightarrow Ca(OH)_2$

2) Calcium hydroxide can also be used in a test for carbon dioxide. If you make a solution of calcium hydroxide in water (called limewater) and bubble gas through it, the solution will turn cloudy if there's carbon dioxide in the gas. The cloudiness is caused by the formation of calcium carbonate.

> calcium hydroxide + carbon dioxide → calcium carbonate + water
> $Ca(OH)_2$ + CO_2 → $CaCO_3$ + H_2O

Limestone — a sea creature's cemetery...

Wow. It sounds like you can achieve pretty much anything with limestone, possibly apart from a bouncy castle. I wonder what we'd be using instead if all those sea creatures hadn't died and conveniently become rock?

Section Five — Acids, Bases and Reaction Rates

Rates of Reaction

Reactions can be fast or slow — you've probably already realised that. But you need to know what affects the rate of a reaction, as well as what you can do to measure it. You'll be on the edge of your seat. Honest.

Reactions Can Go at All Sorts of Different Rates

1) One of the slowest is the rusting of iron (it's not slow enough though — what about my little MGB).
2) A moderate speed reaction is a metal (like magnesium) reacting with acid to produce a gentle stream of bubbles.
3) A really fast reaction is an explosion, where it's all over in a fraction of a second.

The Rate of a Reaction Depends on Four Things:

1) Temperature
2) Concentration — (or pressure for gases)
3) Catalyst
4) Surface area of solids — (or size of solid pieces)

LEARN THEM!

Typical Graphs for Rate of Reaction

The plot below shows how the rate of a particular reaction varies under different conditions. The quickest reaction is shown by the line with the steepest slope. Also, the faster a reaction goes, the sooner it finishes, which means that the line becomes flat earlier.

1) Graph 1 represents the original fairly slow reaction. The graph is not too steep.
2) Graphs 2 and 3 represent the reaction taking place quicker but with the same initial amounts. The slope of the graphs gets steeper.
3) The increased rate could be due to any of these:

   a) increase in temperature
   b) increase in concentration (or pressure)
   c) catalyst added
   d) solid reactant crushed up into smaller bits.

You could also show the amount of reactant used up over time instead — the graphs would have the same shape.

① original reaction
② faster reaction
③ much faster reaction
④ faster, and more reactants

4) Graph 4 produces more product as well as going faster. This can only happen if more reactant(s) are added at the start. Graphs 1, 2 and 3 all converge at the same level, showing that they all produce the same amount of product, although they take different times to get there.

How to get a fast, furious reaction — crack a wee joke...

Industrial reactions generally use a catalyst and are done at high temperature and pressure. Time is money, so the faster an industrial reaction goes the better... but only up to a point. Chemical plants are quite expensive to rebuild if they get blown into lots and lots of teeny tiny pieces.

Section Five — Acids, Bases and Reaction Rates

Measuring Rates of Reaction

Ways to Measure the Rate of a Reaction

The rate of a reaction can be observed either by measuring how quickly the reactants are used up or how quickly the products are formed. It's usually a lot easier to measure products forming.
The rate of reaction can be calculated using the following formula:

$$\text{Rate of Reaction} = \frac{\text{Amount of reactant used or amount of product formed}}{\text{Time}}$$

There are different ways that the rate of a reaction can be measured. Learn these three:

1) Precipitation

1) This is when the product of the reaction is a precipitate which clouds the solution.
2) Observe a mark through the solution and measure how long it takes for it to disappear.
3) The quicker the mark disappears, the quicker the reaction.
4) This only works for reactions where the initial solution is rather see-through.
5) The result is very subjective — different people might not agree over the exact point when the mark 'disappears'.

2) Change in Mass (Usually Gas Given Off)

1) Measuring the speed of a reaction that produces a gas can be carried out on a mass balance.
2) As the gas is released the mass disappearing is easily measured on the balance.
3) The quicker the reading on the balance drops, the faster the reaction.
4) Rate of reaction graphs are particularly easy to plot using the results from this method.
5) This is the most accurate of the three methods described on this page because the mass balance is very accurate. But it has the disadvantage of releasing the gas straight into the room.

3) The Volume of Gas Given Off

1) This involves the use of a gas syringe to measure the volume of gas given off.
2) The more gas given off during a given time interval, the faster the reaction.
3) A graph of gas volume against time elapsed could be plotted to give a rate of reaction graph.
4) Gas syringes usually give volumes accurate to the nearest millilitre, so they're quite accurate. You have to be quite careful though — if the reaction is too vigorous, you can easily blow the plunger out of the end of the syringe!

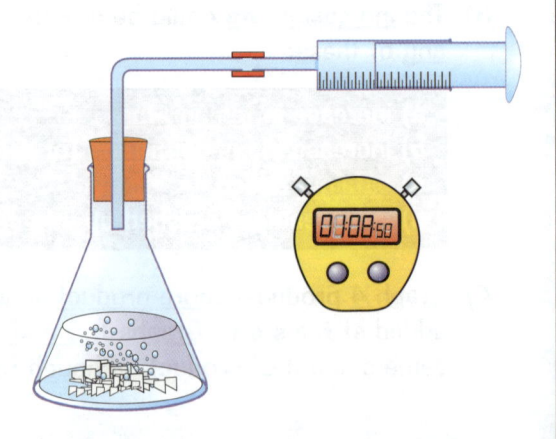

OK have you got your stopwatch ready *BANG!* — oh...

Each method has its pros and cons. The mass balance method is only accurate as long as the flask isn't too hot, otherwise you lose mass by evaporation as well as by the reaction. The first method isn't very accurate, but if you're not producing a gas you can't use either of the other two. Ah well.

Section Five — Acids, Bases and Reaction Rates

Collision Theory

Reaction rates are explained by collision theory. It's really simple. It just says that the rate of a reaction simply depends on how often and how hard the reacting particles collide with each other. The basic idea is that particles have to collide in order to react, and they have to collide hard enough (with enough energy).

More Collisions Increases the Rate of Reaction

The effects of temperature, concentration and surface area on the rate of reaction can be explained in terms of how often the reacting particles collide successfully.

1) HIGHER TEMPERATURE increases collisions

When the temperature is increased the particles all move quicker.
If they're moving quicker, they're going to collide more frequently, and with more energy.

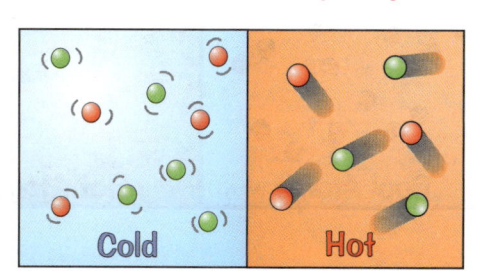

2) HIGHER CONCENTRATION (or PRESSURE) increases collisions

If a solution is made more concentrated it means there are more particles of reactant knocking about between the water molecules which makes collisions between the important particles more likely.
In a gas, increasing the pressure means the particles are more squashed up together so there will be more frequent collisions.

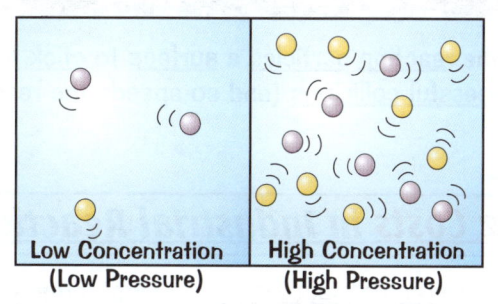

3) LARGER SURFACE AREA increases collisions

If one of the reactants is a solid then breaking it up into smaller pieces will increase the total surface area. This means the particles around it in the solution will have more area to work on, so there'll be more frequent collisions.

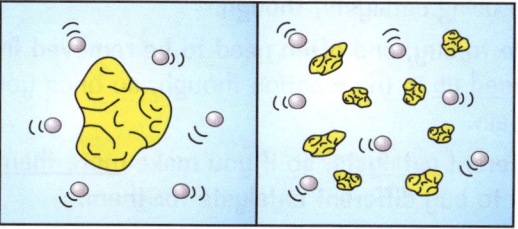

Collision theory — the lamppost ran into me...

Once you've learnt everything off this page, the rates of reaction stuff should start making a lot more sense to you. Isn't it nice when everything starts to fall into place... The concept's fairly simple — the more often particles bump into each other, and the harder they hit when they do, the faster the reaction happens.

Section Five — Acids, Bases and Reaction Rates

Collision Theory and Catalysts

Without enough activation energy, it's game over before you start.

Faster Collisions Increase the Rate of Reaction

Higher temperature also increases the energy of the collisions, because it makes all the particles move faster.

Increasing the temperature causes faster collisions

Reactions only happen if the particles collide with enough energy.
The minimum amount of energy needed by the particles to react is known as the activation energy.
At a higher temperature there will be more particles colliding with enough energy to make the reaction happen.

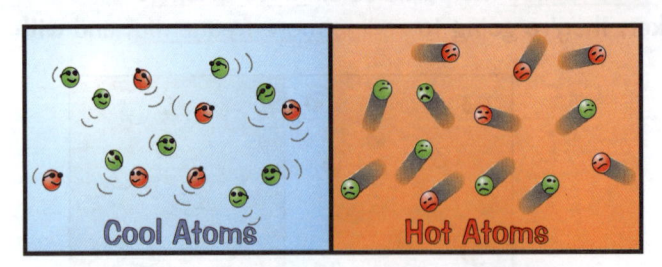

Cool Atoms | Hot Atoms

Catalysts Speed Up Reactions

Many reactions can be speeded up by adding a catalyst.

> A catalyst is a substance which speeds up a reaction, without being changed or used up in the reaction.

A solid catalyst works by giving the reacting particles a surface to stick to.
This increases the number of successful collisions (and so speeds the reaction up).

Catalysts Help Reduce Costs in Industrial Reactions

1) Catalysts are very important for commercial reasons — most industrial reactions use them.
2) Catalysts increase the rate of the reaction, which saves a lot of money simply because the plant doesn't need to operate for as long to produce the same amount of stuff.
3) Alternatively, a catalyst will allow the reaction to work at a much lower temperature. That reduces the energy used up in the reaction (the energy cost), which can save resources and so is better for the environment. It can also save money too.
4) There are disadvantages to using catalysts, though.
5) They can be very expensive to buy, and often need to be removed from the product and cleaned. They never get used up in the reaction though, so once you've got them you can use them over and over again.
6) Different reactions use different catalysts, so if you make more than one product at your plant, you'll probably need to buy different catalysts for them.

Catalysts are like great jokes — they can be used over and over...

And they're not only used in industry... every useful chemical reaction in the human body is catalysed by a biological catalyst (an enzyme). If the reactions in the body were just left to their own devices, they'd take so long to happen, we couldn't exist. Quite handy then, these catalysts.

Section Five — Acids, Bases and Reaction Rates

Revision Summary for Section Five

A good solid section there, if I may say so myself. And who knew acids and alkalis could make such pretty colours. Not so fussed about titrations myself, but you can't expect it all to be sweetness and light. Well here are some more of those nice questions that you enjoy so much. If there are any you can't answer, go back to the appropriate page, do a bit more learning, then try again.

1) What does the pH scale show?
2) What range does the pH scale go from and to? What value is given to a neutral solution?
3) What type of ions are always present in a) acids and   b) alkalis?
4) What is neutralisation? Write down the general equation for neutralisation in terms of ions.
5) What is produced when an acid reacts with a base?
6) What type of reaction is "acid + metal oxide", or "acid + metal hydroxide"?
7) Which acid produces chloride salts when reacting with a base?
8) Suggest a suitable acid and a suitable metal oxide/hydroxide to mix to form the following salts.
   a) copper chloride   b) calcium nitrate   c) zinc sulfate
   d) magnesium nitrate   e) sodium sulfate   f) potassium chloride
9) Write a balanced symbol equation for the reaction between ammonia and nitric acid.
   What is the product of this reaction useful for?
10) Name a suitable indicator you could use in the titration of sulfuric acid and sodium hydroxide.
11)* In a titration, 49 cm^3 of hydrochloric acid was required to neutralise 25cm^3 of sodium hydroxide with a concentration of 0.2 moles per dm^3.
   The equation for the neutralisation reaction is: HCl + NaOH → H$_2$O + NaCl
   Calculate the concentration of the hydrochloric acid in: a) mol/dm^3 b) g/dm^3
12) Why are some metals not suitable for reacting with acids to make soluble salts?
13) How can you tell when a neutralisation reaction is complete if both the base and the salt are soluble in water?
14) Iron chloride can made by mixing iron hydroxide (an insoluble base) with hydrochloric acid. Describe the method you would use to produce pure, solid iron chloride in the lab.
15) Give a practical use of precipitation reactions.
16) Name three uses of limestone.
17) What products are produced when limestone reacts with an acid?
18) What is calcium hydroxide used for?
19) What are the four factors that affect the rate of a reaction?
20) Describe three different ways of measuring the rate of a reaction.
21) A student carries out an experiment to measure the effect of surface area on the reaction between marble and hydrochloric acid. He measures the amount of gas given off at regular intervals.
   a) What factors must he keep constant for it to be a fair test?
   b)* He uses four samples for his experiment:
       Sample A – 10 g of powdered marble
       Sample B – 10 g of small marble chips
       Sample C – 10 g of large marble chips
       Sample D – 5 g of powdered marble
     Sketch a typical set of graphs for this experiment.
22) Explain how higher temperature, higher concentration and larger surface area increase the frequency of successful collisions between particles.
23) What is activation energy?
24) What is the definition of a catalyst?
25) What are the advantages of using catalysts in industrial processes?

* Answers on page 94.

Section Five — Acids, Bases and Reaction Rates

64 Section Six — Crude Oil and Organic Chemistry

Crude Oil

Crude oil is formed from the buried remains of plants and animals — it's a fossil fuel. Over millions of years, the remains turn to crude oil, which can be extracted by drilling and pumping.

Crude Oil is a Mixture of Hydrocarbons

1) A mixture consists of two (or more) elements or compounds that aren't chemically bonded to each other.
2) Crude oil is a mixture of many different compounds. Most of the compounds are hydrocarbon molecules.
3) Hydrocarbons are basically fuels such as petrol and diesel. They're made of only carbon and hydrogen.
4) There are no chemical bonds between the different parts of a mixture, so the different hydrocarbon molecules in crude oil aren't chemically bonded to one another.
5) This means that they all keep their original properties, such as their condensing points. The properties of a mixture are just a mixture of the properties of the separate parts.
6) The parts of the mixture that make up crude oil are known as fractions. These fractions can be separated out by fractional distillation. Each fraction contains molecules with a similar number of carbon atoms to each other (see next page).

Crude Oil is Split into Separate Groups of Hydrocarbons

During fractional distillation, the fractionating column works continuously, with heated crude oil piped in at the bottom. The oil evaporates and rises up the column. The temperature decreases the further up the column you go, so the various fractions are constantly tapped off at the different levels where they condense.

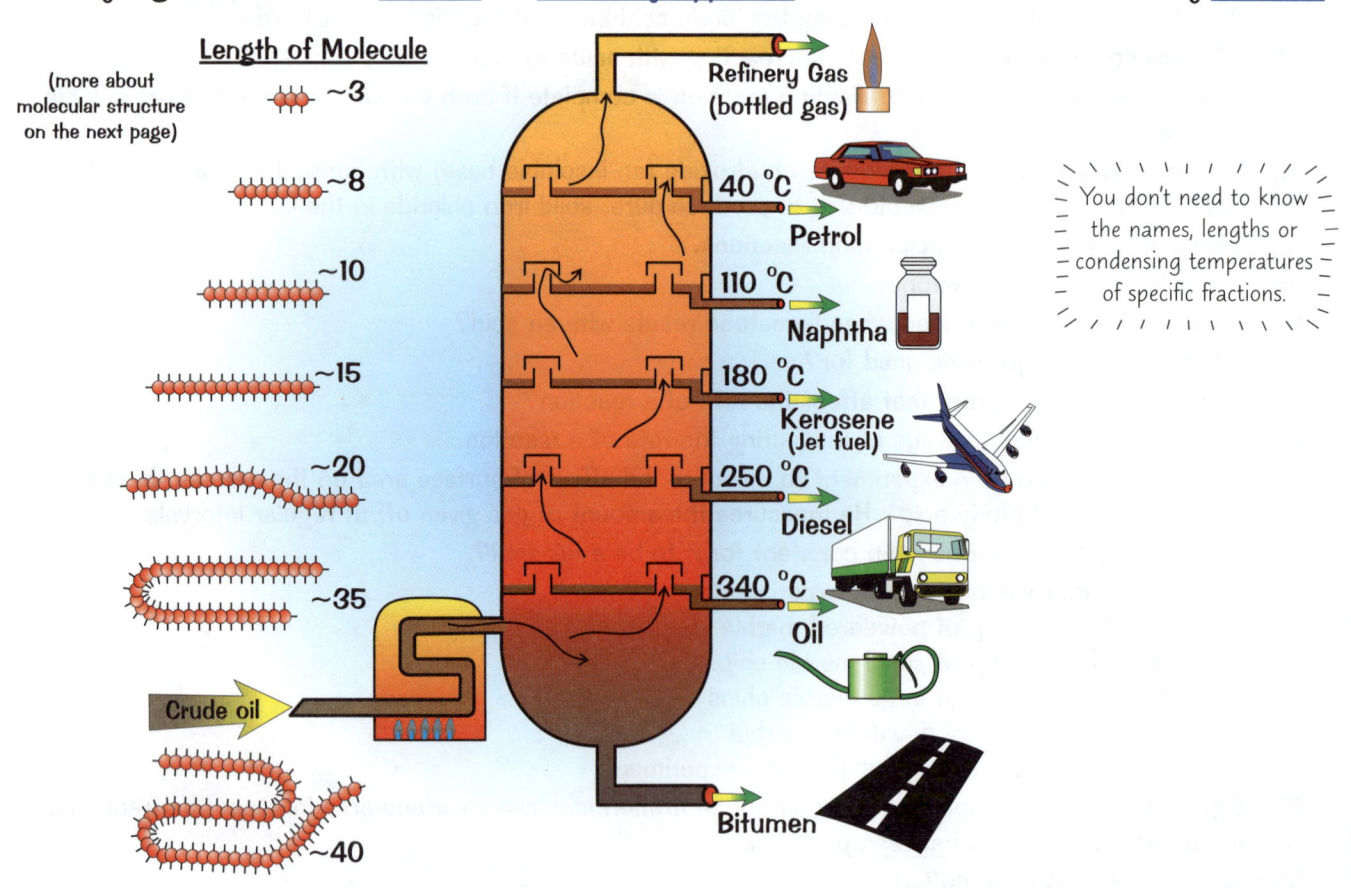

Length of Molecule

(more about molecular structure on the next page)

- ~3
- ~8
- ~10
- ~15
- ~20
- ~35
- ~40

Refinery Gas (bottled gas)
40 °C — Petrol
110 °C — Naphtha
180 °C — Kerosene (Jet fuel)
250 °C — Diesel
340 °C — Oil
Bitumen

Crude oil

You don't need to know the names, lengths or condensing temperatures of specific fractions.

Crude oil — it's always cracking dirty jokes...

It's amazing what you get from buried dead stuff. But it has had a few hundred million years with high temperature and pressure to get into the useful state it's in now. So if we use it all, we're going to have to wait an awfully long time for more to form. No one knows exactly when oil will run out, but some scientists reckon that it could be within this century. The thing is, technology is advancing all the time, so one day it's likely that we'll be able to extract oil that's too difficult and expensive to extract at the moment.

Properties and Uses of Crude Oil

The different fractions of crude oil have different properties, and it's all down to their structure. You need to know the basic structure and a few trends, so you can apply what you've learnt to exam questions.

Crude Oil is Mostly Alkanes

1) Most of the fractions of crude oil are hydrocarbons called alkanes.
2) Alkanes are made up of chains of carbon atoms surrounded by hydrogen atoms.
3) Different alkanes have chains of different lengths.
4) The first three alkanes are methane (natural gas), ethane and propane.

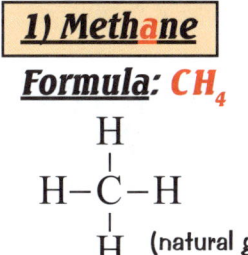

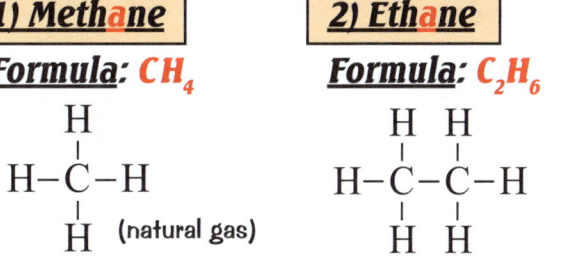

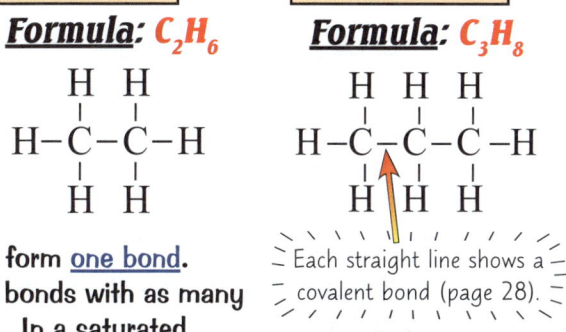

1) Methane
Formula: CH_4

2) Ethane
Formula: C_2H_6

3) Propane
Formula: C_3H_8

Each straight line shows a covalent bond (page 28).

5) Carbon atoms form four bonds and hydrogen atoms only form one bond. The diagrams above show that all the atoms have formed bonds with as many other atoms as they can — this means they're saturated. In a saturated hydrocarbon, all the carbon-carbon bonds are single covalent bonds.
6) The alkanes are a homologous series. This is a group of chemicals that react in a similar way because they have the same general formula. Alkanes all have the general formula C_nH_{2n+2}.
So if an alkane has 5 carbons, it's got to have $(2 \times 5) + 2 = 12$ hydrogens.

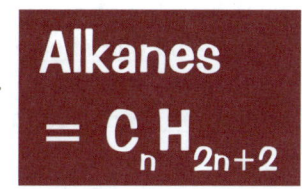

Alkanes = C_nH_{2n+2}

Learn the Basic Trends:

1) The shorter the molecules, the more runny the hydrocarbon is — that is, the less viscous (gloopy) it is.
2) The shorter the molecules, the more volatile they are. "More volatile" means they turn into a gas at a lower temperature. So, the shorter the molecules, the lower the temperature at which that fraction vaporises or condenses — and the lower its boiling point.
3) Also, the shorter the molecules, the more flammable (easier to ignite) the hydrocarbon is.

The Uses Of Hydrocarbons Depend on their Properties

1) The volatility helps decide what the fraction is used for. The refinery gas fraction has the shortest molecules, so it has the lowest boiling point — in fact it's a gas at room temperature. This makes it ideal for using as bottled gas. It's stored under pressure as liquid in 'bottles'. When the tap on the bottle is opened, the fuel vaporises and flows to the burner where it's ignited.
2) The petrol fraction has longer molecules, so it has a higher boiling point. Petrol is a liquid which is ideal for storing in the fuel tank of a car. It can flow to the engine where it's easily vaporised to mix with the air before it is ignited.
3) The viscosity also helps decide how the hydrocarbons are used. The really gloopy, viscous hydrocarbons are used for lubricating engine parts and for covering roads.

Alkane ya if you don't learn this...

So short-chain hydrocarbons are less viscous, more volatile and easier to ignite than longer-chain hydrocarbons. If you learn the properties of short-chain hydrocarbons, you should be able to work out the properties of longer-chain ones in the exam. These properties decide how they're used. In the real world there's more demand for stuff like petrol than there is for long gloopy hydrocarbons like bitumen — I guess there's only so many roads that need covering.

Section Six — Crude Oil and Organic Chemistry

Environmental Problems

We burn fuels all the time to release the energy stored inside them — e.g. 90% of crude oil is used as fuel.

Burning Fossil Fuels Releases Gases and Particles

1) Power stations burn huge amounts of fossil fuels to make electricity. Cars are also a major culprit in burning fossil fuels.
2) Most fuels, such as crude oil and coal, contain carbon and hydrogen. During combustion, the carbon and hydrogen are oxidised so that carbon dioxide and water vapour are released into the atmosphere. Energy (heat) is also produced.
E.g.:

> hydrocarbon + oxygen → carbon dioxide + water vapour

3) If the fuel contains sulfur impurities, the sulfur will be released as sulfur dioxide when the fuel is burnt.
4) Oxides of nitrogen will also form if the fuel burns at a high temperature.
5) When there's plenty of oxygen, all the fuel burns — this is called complete combustion.
6) If there's not enough oxygen, some of the fuel doesn't burn — this is called partial combustion. Under these conditions, solid particles (called particulates) of soot (carbon) and unburnt fuel are released. Carbon monoxide (a poisonous gas) is also released.

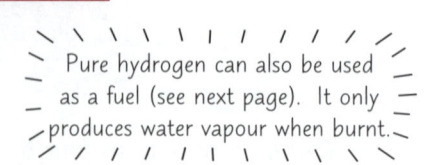

Pure hydrogen can also be used as a fuel (see next page). It only produces water vapour when burnt.

Sulfur Dioxide Causes Acid Rain

1) Sulfur dioxide is one of the gases that causes acid rain.
2) When the sulfur dioxide mixes with clouds it forms dilute sulfuric acid. This then falls as acid rain.
3) In the same way, oxides of nitrogen cause acid rain by forming dilute nitric acid in clouds.
4) Acid rain can cause plants and animals to die and can also damage buildings (see page 58).
5) It has been suggested that it also has links with human health problems.

You can Reduce Acid Rain by Reducing Sulfur Emissions

1) Sulfur can be removed from fuels before they're burnt or from the waste gases that are produced when they're burnt.
2) For example, sulfur is removed from petrol and diesel before it is used in vehicles, and gas scrubbers are used in power stations to remove sulfur from the waste gases after combustion.
3) The other way of reducing acid rain is simply to reduce our usage of fossil fuels.

Eee, problems, problems — there's always summat goin' wrong...

Pollutants like sulfur dioxide can be carried a long way in the atmosphere. So a country might suffer from acid rain that it didn't cause, which doesn't seem very fair. It's not just up to big industries though — there's lots of things you can do to reduce the amount of fossil fuels burnt. Putting an extra jumper on instead of turning up the heating helps. As does walking places instead of cadging a lift.

Section Six — Crude Oil and Organic Chemistry

More Environmental Problems

More doom and gloom on this page I'm afraid... You've got to know it all though.

Increasing Carbon Dioxide Causes Climate Change

1) The level of carbon dioxide in the atmosphere is increasing — because of the large amounts of fossil fuels humans burn.
2) There's a scientific consensus that this extra carbon dioxide has caused the average temperature of the Earth to increase — global warming.
3) Global warming is a type of climate change and causes other types of climate change, e.g. changing rainfall patterns. It could also cause severe flooding due to the polar ice caps melting.

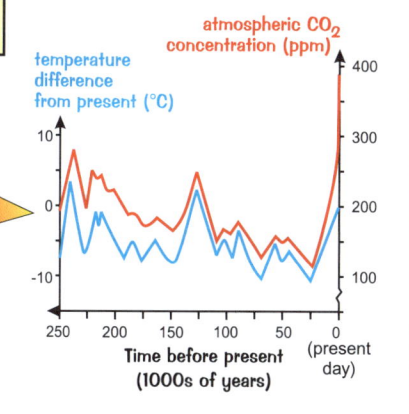

Particles Cause Global Dimming

1) In the last few years, scientists have found that in some areas nearly 25% less sunlight has been reaching the Earth's surface compared to 50 years ago. They have called this global dimming.
2) They think that it's caused by particles of soot and ash that are produced when fossil fuels are burnt. The particles reflect sunlight back into space, or help to produce clouds that reflect sunlight back into space.

Alternative Fuels are Being Developed

Some alternative fuels have already been developed, and there are others in the pipeline (so to speak). Many of them are renewable fuels so, unlike fossil fuels, they won't run out. However, none of them are perfect — they all have pros and cons.

ETHANOL: This is produced from plant material so it's known as a biofuel. It's made by fermenting plant materials at temperatures between 20 and 35 °C to produce a dilute solution of ethanol. Pure ethanol can then be separated from this solution. Ethanol can be mixed with petrol to make a better fuel and is used to power cars in some places.

PROS: The CO_2 released when it's burnt was taken in by the plant as it grew, so it's 'carbon neutral' — it has no carbon footprint. The only other product is water. It's renewable.

CONS: There are worries that as demand for biofuels increases, farmers might start growing crops for biofuel production instead of for food. This could cause an increase in food prices, or even famine. Engines need to be converted before they'll work with ethanol fuels, and ethanol fuel isn't widely available.

BIODIESEL is another type of biofuel. It can be produced from vegetable oils such as rapeseed oil and soybean oil. Biodiesel can be mixed with ordinary diesel fuel and used to run a diesel engine.

PROS: Biodiesel is also 'carbon neutral' and renewable. Engines don't need to be converted. It produces much less sulfur dioxide and 'particulates' than ordinary diesel or petrol.

CONS: We can't make enough to completely replace diesel. It's expensive to make. It could increase food prices like using more ethanol could (see above).

HYDROGEN GAS can also be used to power vehicles. It can be burned as a fuel in combustion engines. It can also be used in fuel cells that are used to power electric vehicles. You get the hydrogen from the electrolysis of water — there's plenty of water about but it takes electrical energy to split it up. This energy could come from a renewable source (e.g. solar), which would reduce the carbon footprint of producing the hydrogen.

PROS: Hydrogen combines with oxygen in the air to form just water — so it's very clean to burn.

CONS: You need a special, expensive engine and hydrogen isn't widely available. You still need to use energy from another source to make it. Also, hydrogen's hard to store.

Global dimming — romantic lighting all day...

Alternative fuels are the shining light at the end of a long tunnel of problems caused by burning fuels (and I mean long). But nothing's perfect (except my quiff... and maybe my golf swing), so get learnin' those disadvantages.

Section Six — Crude Oil and Organic Chemistry

Cracking Crude Oil

After the distillation of crude oil (see page 64), you've still got both short and long hydrocarbons, just not all mixed together. But there's <u>more demand</u> for some products, like <u>petrol</u>, than for others.

Cracking Means Splitting Up Long-chain Hydrocarbons...

1) <u>Long-chain hydrocarbons</u> form <u>thick gloopy liquids</u> like <u>tar</u> which aren't all that useful, so...
2) ... a lot of the longer molecules produced from <u>fractional distillation</u> are <u>turned into smaller ones</u> by a process called <u>cracking</u>.
3) Some of the products of cracking are useful as fuels, e.g. petrol for cars and paraffin for jet fuel.
4) Cracking also produces substances like <u>ethene</u>, which are needed for <u>making plastics</u> (see page 70).

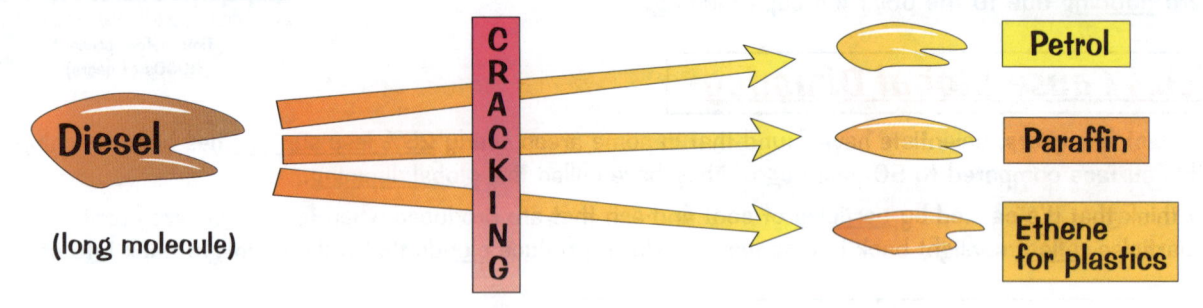

Diesel (long molecule) → CRACKING → Petrol, Paraffin, Ethene for plastics

...by Passing Vapour Over a Hot Catalyst

1) <u>Cracking</u> is a <u>thermal decomposition</u> reaction — <u>breaking molecules down</u> by <u>heating</u> them.
2) The first step is to <u>heat</u> the long-chain hydrocarbon to <u>vaporise</u> it (turn it into a gas).
3) Then the <u>vapour</u> is passed over a <u>powdered catalyst</u> at a temperature of about <u>400 °C – 700 °C</u>.
4) <u>Aluminium oxide</u> is the catalyst used.
5) The <u>long-chain</u> molecules <u>split apart</u> or "crack" on the <u>surface</u> of the specks of catalyst.

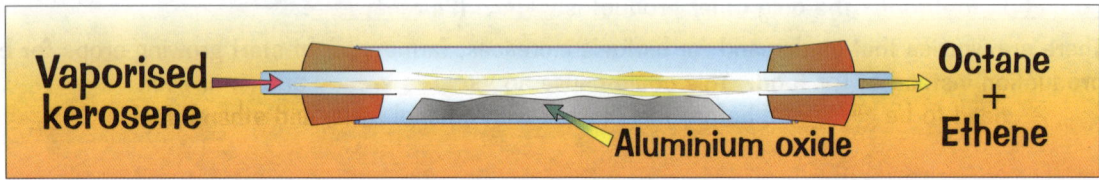

Vaporised kerosene → Aluminium oxide → Octane + Ethene

6) Most of the <u>products</u> of cracking are <u>alkanes</u> (see page 65) and unsaturated hydrocarbons called <u>alkenes</u> (see page 69)...

An alternative way of cracking long-chain hydrocarbons is to mix the vapour with steam at a very high temperature.

Long-chain hydrocarbon molecule → Shorter ALKANE molecule + ALKENE

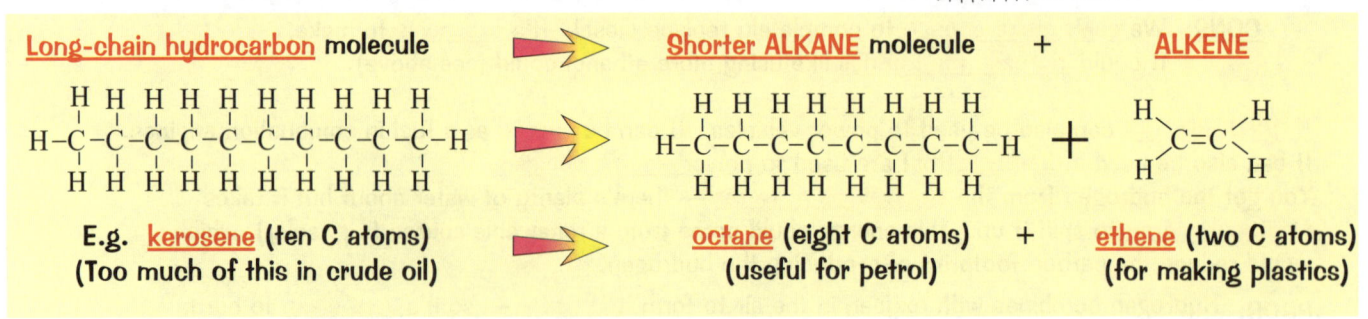

E.g. <u>kerosene</u> (ten C atoms) → <u>octane</u> (eight C atoms) + <u>ethene</u> (two C atoms)
(Too much of this in crude oil) (useful for petrol) (for making plastics)

Get cracking — there's a lot to learn...

Crude oil is <u>useful stuff</u>, but using it is not without its problems. For example, oil is shipped around the planet, which can lead to <u>slicks</u> if there's an accident. Also, burning oil is thought to cause <u>climate change</u>, <u>acid rain</u> and <u>global dimming</u>. Oil is going to start <u>running out</u> one day, which will lead to big difficulties.

Section Six — Crude Oil and Organic Chemistry

Alkenes and Ethanol

Alkenes are very useful. You can use them to make all sorts of stuff.

Alkenes Have a C=C Double Bond

1) Alkenes are hydrocarbons which have a double covalent bond between two of the carbon atoms in their chain.
2) They are known as unsaturated because they can make more bonds — the double bond can open up, allowing the two carbon atoms to bond with other atoms.
3) The first two alkenes are ethene (with two carbon atoms) and propene (three Cs).

1) Ethene
Formula: C_2H_4

Carbon atoms always make four bonds, but hydrogen atoms only make one.

This is a double bond — so each carbon atom is still making four bonds.

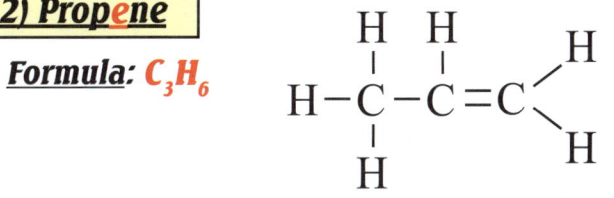

2) Propene
Formula: C_3H_6

Alkenes = C_nH_{2n}

4) The alkenes are a homologous series (see page 65). They have the general formula: C_nH_{2n} — they have twice as many hydrogens as carbons.

You Can Test for an Alkene using Bromine Water

1) Add the unknown substance to bromine water.
2) An alkene will decolourise the bromine water, turning it from orange to colourless.
3) This is because the double bond has opened up and formed bonds with the bromine.

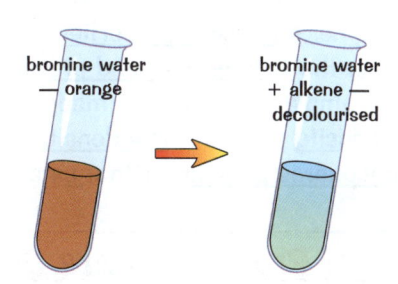

Ethanol Can Be Produced from Ethene and Steam

1) Ethene is produced from crude oil (by cracking — see page 68).
2) Ethene (C_2H_4) will react with steam (H_2O) to make ethanol.
3) The reaction needs a temperature of 300 °C and a pressure of 60-70 atmospheres.
4) Phosphoric acid is used as a catalyst.

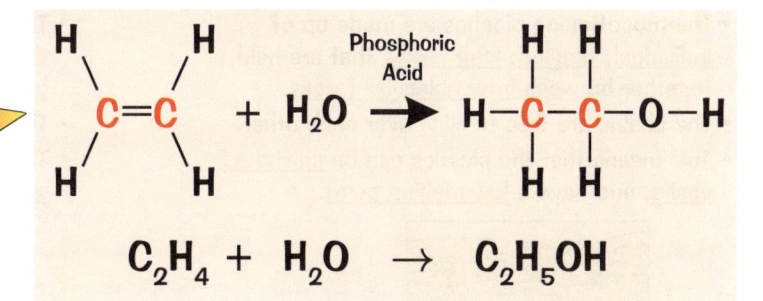

$C_2H_4 + H_2O \rightarrow C_2H_5OH$

Glad to see you're alkene for a bit of organic chemistry...

Don't get alkenes confused with alkanes — that one letter makes all the difference. Alkenes have a double covalent bond, alkanes don't. But the first part of both their names tells you how many C atoms they have. "Meth-" means "one carbon atom", "eth-" means "two C atoms", and "prop-" means "three C atoms". And remember — alkenes decolourise bromine water and alkanes don't.

Section Six — Crude Oil and Organic Chemistry

Polymers

Before we knew how to make polymers, there were no polythene bags. Everyone used string bags for their shopping. Now we have plastic bags that hurt your hands and split halfway home.

Alkenes Can Be Used to Make Polymers

1) Probably the most useful thing you can do with alkenes is polymerisation. This means joining together lots of small alkene molecules (monomers) to form very large molecules — these long-chain molecules are called polymers.

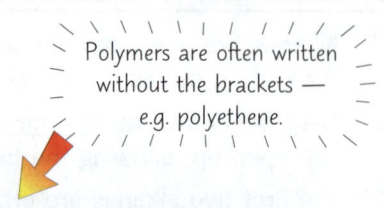

2) For instance, many ethene molecules can be joined up to produce poly(ethene) or "polythene".

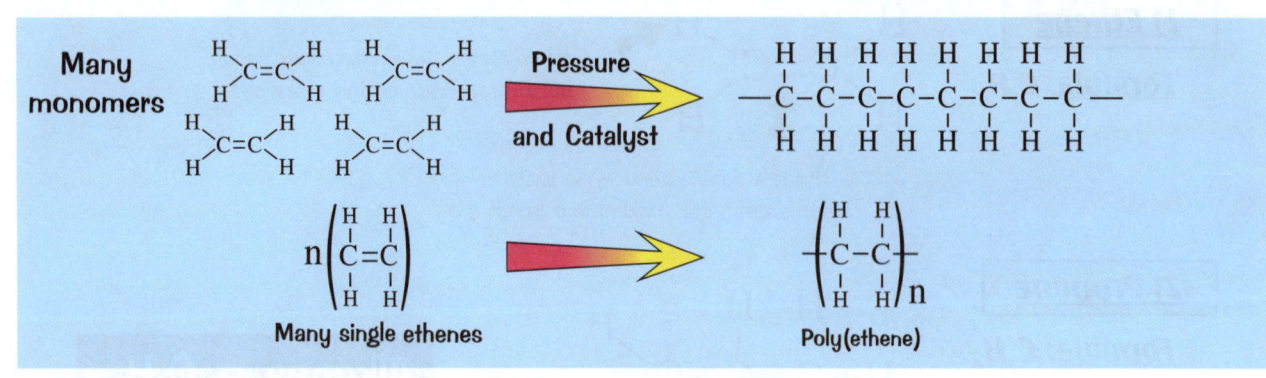

Polymers are often written without the brackets — e.g. polyethene.

Many monomers → Pressure and Catalyst → Poly(ethene)

3) In the same way, if you join lots of propene molecules together, you've got poly(propene).

Different Polymers Have Different Physical Properties

1) The physical properties of a polymer depend on what it's made from. Polyamides are usually stronger than poly(ethene), for example.

2) A polymer's physical properties are also affected by the conditions it's made under — e.g. the temperature and pressure of polymerisation, and the type of catalyst used. For example, poly(ethene) made at 200 °C and 2000 atmospheres pressure is flexible, and has low density — this is low density (LD) poly(ethene). But poly(ethene) made at 60 °C and a few atmospheres pressure with a catalyst is rigid and dense — this is high density (HD) poly(ethene).

Physical Properties are Determined by the Forces Between Molecules

Strong covalent bonds hold the atoms together in polymer chains. But it's the forces between the different chains that determine the properties of the plastic.

Thermosoftening plastics:
- Thermosoftening plastics are made up of individual, tangled, long chains that are held together by weak intermolecular forces.
- The chains are free to slide over each other.
- This means that the plastics can be stretched easily, and have a low melting point.

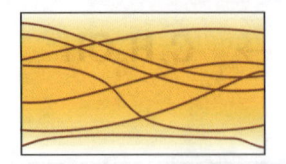

Thermosetting plastics:
- Thermosetting plastics have stronger bonds between the polymer chains — these might be covalent bonds between the chains, or cross-linking bridges.
- The crosslinks hold the chains firmly together.
- This means these plastics are rigid and can't be stretched, and have higher melting points.

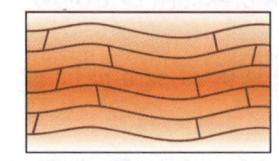

Polly Murs? Sounds like a singing parrot...

Which monomer a polymer is made from affects the properties of the plastic, which also affects what the plastic can be used for (more on this on the next page, in case you're interested). For this page, you also need to be completely sure about what a monomer is and what this polymerisation malarkey is all about.

Section Six — Crude Oil and Organic Chemistry

More on Polymers

Polymers are dead useful for all sorts of things — but they have their downsides too.
Unfortunately they're pretty stubborn, which makes them difficult to get rid of after they've been used.

There are Loads of Different Uses for Polymers

Polymers are everywhere. They've been used for ages to make things like:

1) Plastic bags — which are made from light, stretchable polymers such as low density poly(ethene).
2) Tights — the super-stretchy LYCRA® fibre you get in tights is made from elastic polymer fibres.

But new uses are being developed all the time too. Examples are:

1) New biodegradable packaging materials made from polymers and cornstarch.
2) Waterproof coatings for fabrics.
3) Dental polymers that are used in resin tooth fillings.
4) Polymer hydrogel wound dressings that keep wounds moist.
5) Hydrogels that are used in contact lenses because they're flexible.  
6) Polymers that are used to make smart materials, such as memory foam. Memory foam is a polymer that gets softer as it gets warmer. Mattresses can be made of memory foam — they mould to your body shape when you lie on them. (See page 51 for more on smart materials.)

Polymers Are Cheap, but Most Don't Rot — They're Hard to Get Rid Of

1) Most polymers aren't "biodegradable" — they're not broken down by microorganisms, so they don't rot.
2) This means that it's difficult to get rid of them, which can cause problems with litter. Also, even if you bury them in a landfill site, they'll still be there years later. The best thing is to re-use them as many times as possible and then recycle them if you can.
3) Things made from polymers are usually cheaper than things made from metal. However, as crude oil resources get used up, the price of crude oil will rise. Crude oil products like polymers will get dearer.
4) It may be that one day there won't be enough oil for fuel AND plastics AND all the other uses. Choosing how to use the oil that's left means weighing up advantages and disadvantages on all sides.

Biodegradeable Plastics Can Be Used Instead

1) It's possible to include extra stuff like cornstarch in plastic products. Cornstarch makes the polymers break down more quickly.
2) Biodegradable plastics made from cornstarch have already been developed, and are used in carrier bags and food packaging.

Revision's like a polymer — you join lots of little facts up...

Polymers are all over the place — and I don't just mean all those plastic bags stuck in trees. There are naturally occurring polymers, like rubber and silk. That's quite a few clothing options, even without synthetic polymers like polyester and PVC. You've even got polymers on the inside — DNA's a polymer.

Section Six — Crude Oil and Organic Chemistry

Alcohols

This page is about different types of alcohols — and that's not just beer, wine and spirits.

Alcohols Have an '-OH' Functional Group and End in '-ol'

1) The general formula of an alcohol is $C_nH_{2n+1}OH$. So an alcohol with 2 carbons has the formula C_2H_5OH.
2) All alcohols contain the same -OH group. You need to know the first 3 in the homologous series:

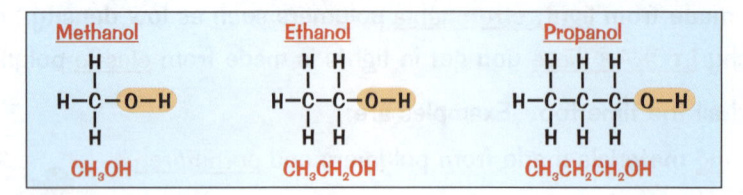

Methanol — CH_3OH
Ethanol — CH_3CH_2OH
Propanol — $CH_3CH_2CH_2OH$

3) The basic naming system is the same as for alkanes — but replace the final '-e' with '-ol'.
4) Don't write CH_4O instead of CH_3OH — it doesn't show the functional -OH group.

The First Three Alcohols Have Similar Properties

1) Alcohols are flammable. They burn in air to produce carbon dioxide and water. E.g.

$$2CH_3OH_{(l)} + 3O_{2(g)} \rightarrow 2CO_{2(g)} + 4H_2O_{(g)}$$

2) The first three alcohols all dissolve completely in water to form neutral solutions.
3) They also react with sodium to produce hydrogen. E.g.

$$2C_2H_5OH_{(l)} + 2Na_{(s)} \rightarrow 2C_2H_5ONa_{(aq)} + H_{2(g)}$$

4) Ethanol is the main alcohol in alcoholic drinks. It's not as toxic as methanol (which causes blindness if drunk) but it still damages the liver and brain.

Alcohols are Used as Solvents

1) Alcohols such as methanol and ethanol can dissolve most compounds that water dissolves, but they can also dissolve substances that water can't dissolve — e.g. hydrocarbons, oils and fats. This makes ethanol, methanol and propanol very useful solvents in industry.
2) Ethanol is the solvent for perfumes and aftershave lotions. It can mix with both the oils (which give the smell) and the water (that makes up the bulk).
3) 'Methylated spirit' (or 'meths') is ethanol with chemicals (e.g. methanol) added to it. It's used to clean paint brushes and as a fuel (among other things). It's poisonous to drink, so a purply-blue dye is also added (to stop people drinking it by mistake).

Alcohols are Used as Fuels

1) Ethanol is used as a fuel in spirit burners — it burns fairly cleanly and it's non-smelly.
2) Ethanol can also be mixed in with petrol and used as fuel for cars (see page 67). Since pure ethanol is clean burning, the more ethanol in a petrol/ethanol mix, the less pollution is produced.
3) Some countries that have little or no oil deposits but plenty of land and sunshine (e.g. Brazil) grow loads of sugar cane, which they ferment to form ethanol.
4) A big advantage of this is that sugar cane is a renewable resource (unlike petrol, which will run out).

Quick tip — don't fill your car with single malt whisky...

The examiners will be happy if you know the formulas, the structures, the properties and the reactions on this page. They might also give you some extra information about alcohols to evaluate... knowing the facts on this page will help you be able to do that. I know what I'd do...

Section Six — Crude Oil and Organic Chemistry

Carboxylic Acids

So what if carboxylic is a funny name — these are easy.

Carboxylic Acids Have the Functional Group -COOH

1) Carboxylic acids have '-COOH' as a functional group.

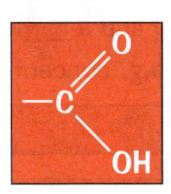

2) Their names end in '-anoic acid' (and start with the normal 'meth/eth/prop'). These are the first three in the homologous series:

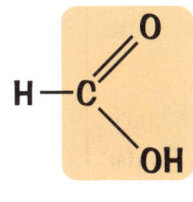

Methanoic acid
HCOOH

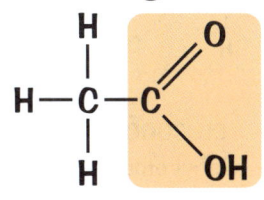

Ethanoic acid
CH_3COOH

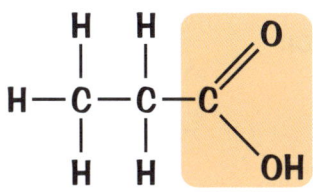

Propanoic acid
CH_3CH_2COOH

Carboxylic Acids React in Many Ways

1) They react just like any other acid with carbonates to produce a salt, carbon dioxide and water.
2) The salts formed in these reactions end in -anoate — e.g. methanoic acid will form a methanoate, ethanoic acid an ethanoate, etc. For example:

> ethanoic acid + sodium carbonate → carbon dioxide + water + sodium ethanoate
> $2CH_3COOH_{(aq)} + Na_2CO_{3(s)} → CO_{2(g)} + H_2O_{(l)} + 2CH_3COONa_{(aq)}$

3) Carboxylic acids dissolve in water to produce acidic solutions.
   - When they dissolve, they ionise and release H^+ ions which are responsible for making the solution acidic.
   - But, because they don't ionise completely (not many H^+ ions are released), they just form weak acidic solutions.
   - This means that they have a higher pH (less acidic) than aqueous solutions of strong acids with the same concentration.

> The strength of an acid isn't the same as its concentration. Concentration is how watered down your acid is and strength is how well it has ionised in water.

4) Carboxylic acids are also used in the preparation of esters. Carboxylic acids react with alcohols in the presence of an acid catalyst to form esters — there's more on this on the next page.

Vinegar Contains a Carboxylic Acid

1) Ethanoic acid can be made by oxidising ethanol. Microbes, like yeast, cause the ethanol to ferment. Ethanol can also be oxidised using oxidising agents.

> ethanol + oxygen → ethanoic acid + water

If you leave wine open, the ethanol in it is oxidised — this is why it goes off.

2) Ethanoic acid can then be dissolved in water to make vinegar, which is used for flavouring and preserving foods.

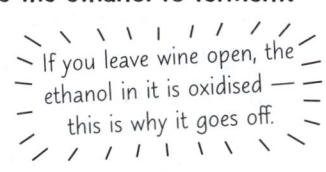

Ethanoic acid — it's not just for putting on your chips...

The trickiest bit on this page is probably the bit about carboxylic acids not ionising completely in water and being weak acids. But when it comes to carbonates, they just act like any old acid — easy.

Section Six — Crude Oil and Organic Chemistry

Esters

Mix an alcohol from p.72 and a carboxylic acid from p.73, and what have you got... an ester, that's what.

Esters Have the Functional Group -COO-

1) Esters are formed from an alcohol and a carboxylic acid.
2) An acid catalyst is usually used (e.g. concentrated sulfuric acid).

alcohol + carboxylic acid → ester + water

CH_3COOH Ethanoic acid
CH_3CH_2OH Ethanol
$CH_3COOCH_2CH_3$ Ethyl ethanoate
H_2O Water

Their names end in '-oate'.
The alcohol forms the first part of the ester's name, and the acid forms the second part.

ethanol + ethanoic acid → ethyl ethanoate + water
methanol + propanoic acid → methyl propanoate + water

Esters Smell Nice but Don't Mix Well with Water

1) Many esters have pleasant smells — often quite sweet and fruity. They're also volatile. This makes them ideal for perfumes (the evaporated molecules can be detected by smell receptors in your nose).
2) However, many esters are flammable (or even highly flammable). So their volatility also makes them potentially dangerous.
3) Esters don't mix very well with water. (They're not nearly as soluble as alcohols or carboxylic acids.)
4) But esters do mix well with alcohols and other organic solvents.

Esters are Often Used in Flavourings and Perfumes

1) Because many esters smell nice, they're used in perfumes.
2) Esters are also used to make flavourings and aromas — e.g. there are esters that smell or taste of rum, apple, orange, banana, grape, pineapple, etc.
3) Some esters are used in ointments (they give Deep Heat® its smell).
4) Other esters are used as solvents for paint, ink, glue and in nail varnish remover.

There are things you need to think about when using esters:

1) Inhaling the fumes from some esters irritates mucous membranes in the nose and mouth.
2) Ester fumes are heavier than air and very flammable. Flammable vapour + naked flame = flash fire.
3) Some esters are toxic, especially in large doses. Some people worry about health problems associated with synthetic food additives such as esters.
4) BUT... esters aren't as volatile or as toxic as some other organic solvents — they don't release nearly as many toxic fumes as some of them. In fact esters have replaced solvents such as toluene in many paints and varnishes.

What's a chemist's favourite chocolate — ester eggs...

Who'd have thought those pear drops your gran's such a fan of contained esters instead of pears? It's a crazy old world. Make sure you're clued up on esters before you turn the page.

Section Six — Crude Oil and Organic Chemistry

Revision Summary for Section Six

So there you go. Stuff from every part of life covered in one section — petrol, plastic bags, vinegar, pear drops and impending environmental doom. I don't know about you but I need a sit down. (Actually, I'm already sitting down — what I really need is a lovely nap, but duty calls.) Anyway, as you might be aware by now, it's traditional at these times to have a go at a few questions — so here they are...

1) What does crude oil consist of? What does fractional distillation do to crude oil?
2) What is a homologous series?
3) What's the general formula for an alkane?
4) Is a short-chain hydrocarbon more viscous than a long-chain hydrocarbon? Is it more volatile?
5)* You're going on holiday to a very cold place. The temperature will be about –10 °C. Which of the fuels shown on the right do you think will work best in your camping stove? Explain your answer.

Fuel	Boiling point (°C)
Propane	–42
Butane	–0.4
Pentane	36.2

6) Name three pollutants released into the atmosphere when fossil fuels are burned. What environmental problems are associated with each?
7) List three ways of reducing acid rain.
8) What is global dimming?
9) List three alternative ways of powering cars. What are the pros and cons of each?
10) What is "cracking"? Why is it done?
11) Give a typical example of a substance that is cracked, and the products that you get from cracking it.
12) What kind of carbon-carbon bond do alkenes have?
13) Draw the chemical structure of ethene.
14) What is the general formula for alkenes?
15) When ethene is hydrated with steam, what substance is formed?
16) What are polymers? What kinds of substances can form polymers?
17) Give two factors which affect the physical properties of a polymer.
18) What are the differences between thermosoftening and thermosetting plastics?
19) List four 'new' uses of polymers.
20) Why might polymers become more expensive in the future?
21) What substance can you add to plastic products to make them biodegradable?
22) Draw the structure of the first three alcohols.
23) When alcohols dissolve in water, is the solution acidic, neutral or alkaline?
24) What gas is formed when alcohols react with sodium?
25) What is the functional group in carboxylic acids?
26) What gas is produced when carboxylic acids react with carbonates?
27) Why are carboxylic acids weak acids?
28) How is vinegar made?
29) What two kinds of substance react together to form an ester? What catalyst is used in the formation of esters?
30) Write down two uses of esters.

*Answers on page 94.

Section Six — Crude Oil and Organic Chemistry

Section Seven — Energy and Equilibria

Energy Transfer in Reactions

In a chemical reaction, energy can be transferred to or from the surroundings, and it's all about making and breaking bonds.

Energy Must Always be Supplied to Break Bonds

1) During a chemical reaction, old bonds are broken and new bonds are formed.
2) Energy must be supplied to break existing bonds — so bond breaking is an endothermic process.
3) Energy is released when new bonds are formed — so bond formation is an exothermic process.

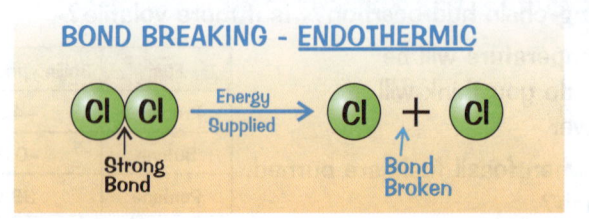

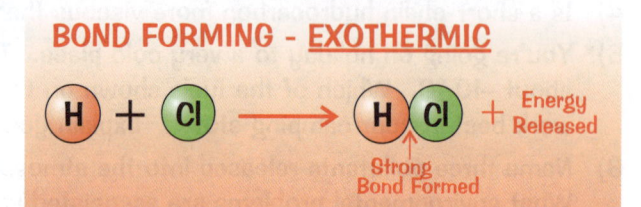

BOND BREAKING - ENDOTHERMIC

Cl Cl → (Energy Supplied) → Cl + Cl
Strong Bond → Bond Broken

BOND FORMING - EXOTHERMIC

H + Cl → H Cl + Energy Released
Strong Bond Formed

In an Exothermic Reaction, Energy is Given Out

In an EXOTHERMIC reaction, the energy released in bond formation is greater than the energy used in breaking old bonds.

> An **EXOTHERMIC reaction** is one which **GIVES OUT ENERGY** to the surroundings, usually in the form of heat and usually shown by a **RISE IN TEMPERATURE**.

In an Endothermic Reaction, Energy is Taken In

In an ENDOTHERMIC reaction, the energy required to break old bonds is greater than the energy released when new bonds are formed.

> An **ENDOTHERMIC reaction** is one which **TAKES IN ENERGY** from the surroundings, usually in the form of heat and usually shown by a **FALL IN TEMPERATURE**.

The Change in Energy is Called the Enthalpy Change

> The overall change in energy in a reaction is called the **ENTHALPY** change. It has the symbol ΔH.

Δ is the Greek letter 'delta'. It means 'change in'. The H means enthalpy.

1) The units of ΔH are kJ/mol — so it's the amount of energy in kilojoules per mole of reactant.
2) Enthalpy change can have a positive value or a negative value.
   - If the reaction is exothermic, the value is negative because the reaction is giving out energy.
   - If the reaction is endothermic, the value is positive because the reaction takes in energy.

Right, so burning gives out heat — really...

This whole energy transfer thing is a fairly simple idea — don't be put off by the long words. Remember, "exo-" = exit, "-thermic" = heat, so an exothermic reaction is one that gives out heat. And "endo-" = erm... the other one. Okay, so there's no easy way to remember that one. Tough.

Energy Transfers and Reversible Reactions

Some reactions are endothermic, some are exothermic and reversible reactions can be both.

In an Exothermic Reaction, Heat is Given Out

1) The best example of an exothermic reaction is burning fuels — also called COMBUSTION. This gives out a lot of heat — it's very exothermic.
2) Neutralisation reactions (acid + alkali — see page 53) are also exothermic.
3) Many oxidation reactions are exothermic. For example, adding sodium to water produces heat, so it must be exothermic. The sodium emits heat and moves about on the surface of the water as it is oxidised (see page 41).
4) Exothermic reactions have lots of everyday uses. For example, some hand warmers use the exothermic oxidation of iron in air (with a salt solution catalyst) to generate heat. Self heating cans of hot chocolate and coffee also rely on exothermic reactions between chemicals in their bases.

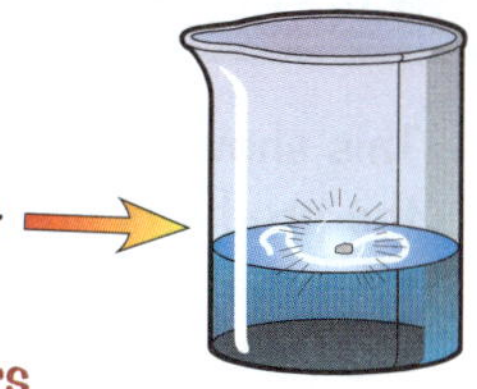

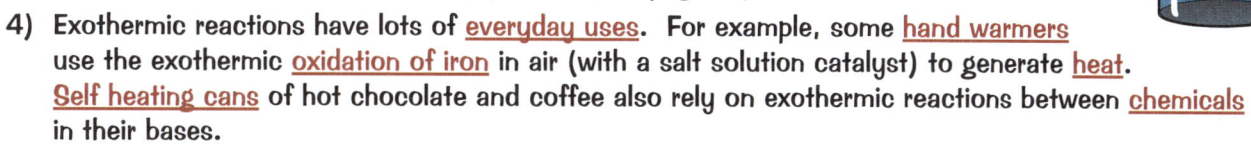

In an Endothermic Reaction, Heat is Taken In

Endothermic reactions are much less common. Thermal decompositions are a good example:

> Heat must be supplied to make calcium carbonate decompose to make quicklime.
> $$CaCO_3 \rightarrow CaO + CO_2$$

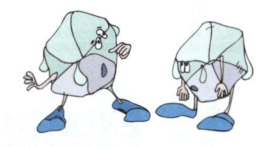

Endothermic reactions also have everyday uses. For example, some sports injury packs use endothermic reactions — they take in heat and the pack becomes very cold. More convenient than carrying ice around.

Reversible Reactions Can Be Endothermic and Exothermic

In reversible reactions (see page 24), if the reaction is endothermic in one direction, it will be exothermic in the other direction. The energy absorbed by the endothermic reaction is equal to the energy released during the exothermic reaction. A good example is the thermal decomposition of hydrated copper sulfate.

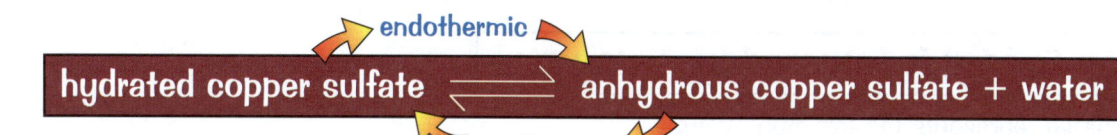

> endothermic
> hydrated copper sulfate ⇌ anhydrous copper sulfate + water
> exothermic

"Anhydrous" just means "without water", and "hydrated" means "with water".

1) If you heat blue hydrated copper(II) sulfate crystals it drives the water off and leaves white anhydrous copper(II) sulfate powder. This is endothermic.

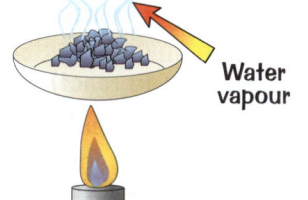

2) If you then add a couple of drops of water to the white powder you get the blue crystals back again. This is exothermic.

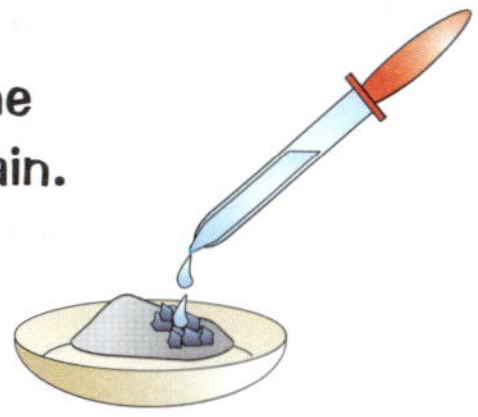

Right... so burning still gives out heat — gotcha...

So there are quite a few different examples of exothermic and endothermic reactions, although endothermic are more unusual. Shame I don't have an exothermic mug for my tea... it'd be great for when I've been so busy writing chemistry that I've let it go cold. Cold tea is just not cool. Well technically it is but you get the idea...

Section Seven — Energy and Equilibria

Energy Level Diagrams

Energy level diagrams show how the energy levels of the reactants change when they react to form the products.

Energy Level Diagrams Show if it's Exo- or Endo-thermic

In exothermic reactions ΔH is –ve
ΔH is the enthalpy change (see page 76).

1) This shows an exothermic reaction — the products are at a lower energy than the reactants.
2) The difference in height represents the energy given out in the reaction (per mole). ΔH is –ve here.
3) The initial rise in the line represents the energy needed to break the old bonds. This is the activation energy.

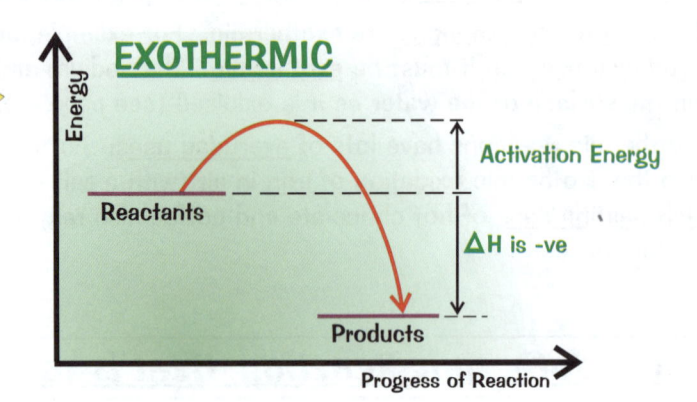

In endothermic reactions ΔH is +ve

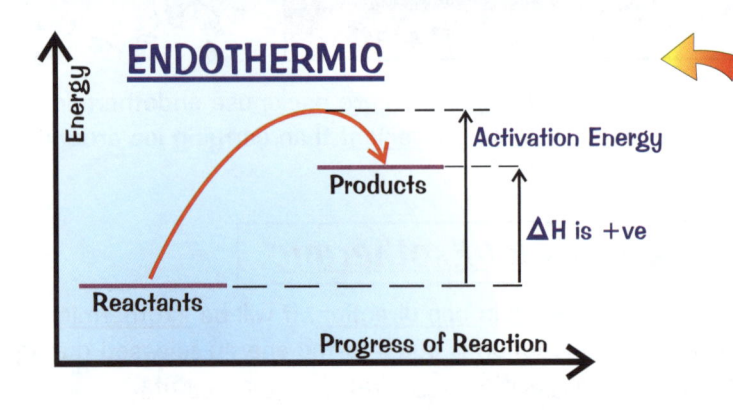

1) This shows an endothermic reaction because the products are at a higher energy than the reactants, so ΔH is +ve.
2) The difference in height represents the energy taken in during the reaction.

The Activation Energy is Lowered by Catalysts

1) The activation energy represents the minimum energy needed by reacting particles for the reaction to occur.
2) A catalyst makes reactions happen faster by providing an alternative reaction pathway (i.e another way for the particles to react) with a lower activation energy.
3) This is represented by the lower curve on the diagram, which shows that less initial energy is needed for the reaction to begin.
4) The overall energy change (or enthalpy change) for the reaction, ΔH, remains the same though.

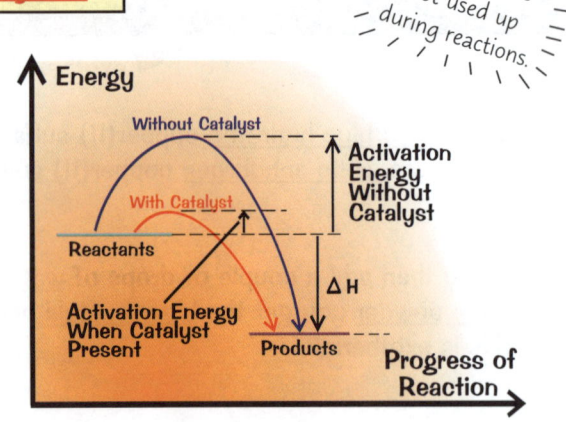

Catalysts are not used up during reactions.

Energy transfer — make sure you take it all in...

So for exothermic reactions, there's a step down on the energy level diagram 'cause the products have less energy than the reactants. In endothermic reactions, it's the other way round — there's a step up from reactants to products. And catalysts handily reduce the activation energy needed to kick off a reaction. Sorted.

Section Seven — Energy and Equilibria

Bond Dissociation Energy

You can <u>calculate</u> the <u>enthalpy change</u> for a reaction by looking at the bonds that are made and broken.

Bond Dissociation Energy — The Amount of Energy in a Bond

1) <u>Each type</u> of chemical bond (e.g. C–C or C–H) has a particular <u>bond dissociation energy</u> associated with it.
2) This <u>bond dissociation energy</u> can vary slightly depending what <u>compound</u> the bond is in — so you'll be given <u>average bond dissociation energies</u> in the exam.
3) You can use these to calculate the <u>enthalpy</u> change for a reaction. The basic idea is really simple — <u>add up</u> the energy of the bonds that are <u>broken</u> and <u>subtract</u> the energy of the bonds that are <u>made</u>.

Example: The Formation of HCl

Using bond dissociation energies you can <u>calculate</u> the <u>enthalpy change</u> for this reaction:

$$H_2 + Cl_2 \rightarrow 2HCl$$

The bond dissociation energies you need are:
- H–H: +436 kJ/mol
- Cl–Cl: +242 kJ/mol
- H–Cl: +431 kJ/mol

1) <u>BREAKING one mole</u> of H–H and one mole of Cl–Cl bonds <u>requires</u>:
   $$436 + 242 = \underline{678 \text{ kJ}}$$

2) <u>FORMING two moles</u> of H–Cl bonds <u>releases</u>:
   $$2 \times 431 = \underline{862 \text{ kJ}}$$

3) Then use this formula to calculate the difference:

   > Enthalpy change (ΔH) = Total energy absorbed to break bonds − Total energy released in making bonds

4) So, $\Delta H = 678 - 862 = \underline{-184 \text{ kJ/mol}}$

5) The ΔH is <u>negative</u>, so the reaction must be <u>exothermic</u>.

You can even draw all this out on an <u>energy level diagram</u>:

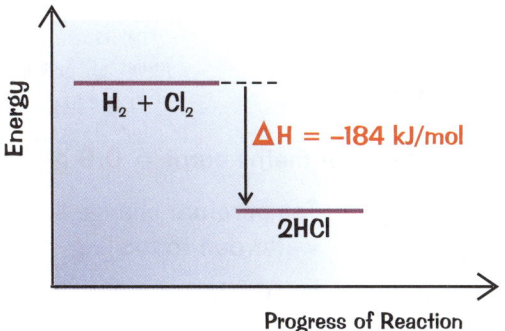

When you're drawing an energy level diagram don't forget to label the reactants, products, ΔH and the axes.

[Energy level diagram showing H₂ + Cl₂ at higher energy, dropping by $\Delta H = -184$ kJ/mol to 2HCl; axes labelled Energy vs Progress of Reaction]

You might get given a slightly <u>more complicated</u> reaction where there are more bonds to break and make, but the method is <u>just the same</u>.

> For example in the reaction:
> $$CH_4 + 2O_2 \rightarrow CO_2 + 2H_2O$$
> There are <u>4 × C–H</u> bonds broken, <u>2 × O=O</u> bonds broken, <u>2 × C=O</u> bonds made and <u>4 × O–H</u> bonds made.

"The name's Bond, C–H Bond..." — sorry, I couldn't help it...

These calculations might look scary but really they're quite straightforward. Whatever the reaction is, the method is <u>always the same</u> — calculate the energy of <u>all the bonds that are broken</u> and the energy of <u>all the bonds that are made</u>, then plug them in the <u>formula</u>. Voilà. Then sit back and be proud you've mastered enthalpy change.

Measuring Energy Transfer

Energy Transfer can be Measured

1) You can measure the amount of <u>energy released</u> by an exothermic <u>chemical reaction</u> (in solution) by taking the <u>temperature of the reagents</u> (making sure they're the same), <u>mixing</u> them in a <u>polystyrene cup</u> and measuring the <u>temperature of the solution</u> at the <u>end</u> of the reaction. Easy.

2) The biggest <u>problem</u> with energy measurements is the amount of energy <u>lost to the surroundings</u>.

3) You can reduce it a bit by putting the polystyrene cup into a <u>beaker of cotton wool</u> to give <u>more insulation</u>, and putting a <u>lid</u> on the cup to reduce energy lost by <u>evaporation</u>.

4) This method works for reactions of <u>solids with water</u> (e.g. dissolving ammonium nitrate in water) as well as for <u>neutralisation</u> reactions.

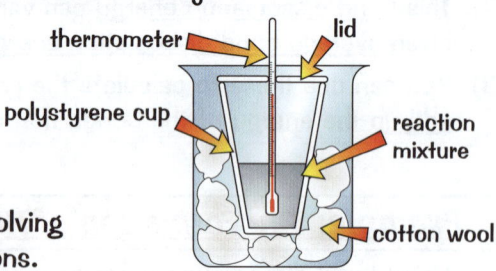

1) Place 25 cm³ of 1 mol/dm³ hydrochloric acid in a polystyrene cup, and record its temperature.
2) Put 25 cm³ of 1 mol/dm³ sodium hydroxide in a measuring cylinder and record its temperature.
3) As long as they're at the same temperature, add the alkali to the acid and stir.
4) Take the temperature of the mixture every 30 seconds, and record the highest temperature it reaches.

This method can also be used for endothermic reactions — there will be a fall in temperature.

Fuel Energy is Calculated Using Calorimetry

Different fuels produce <u>different amounts of energy</u>. To measure the amount of energy released when a fuel is burnt, you can simply burn the fuel and use the flame to <u>heat up some water</u>. Of course, this has to have a fancy chemistry name — <u>calorimetry</u>. Calorimetry uses a <u>glass</u> or <u>metal container</u> (it's usually made of <u>copper</u> because copper conducts heat so well).

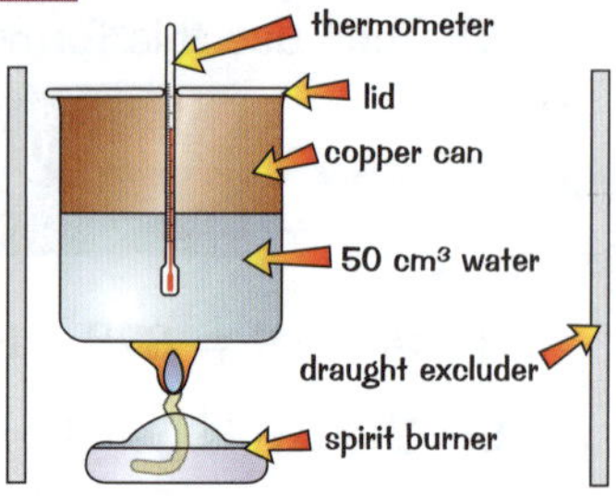

Method:

1) Put 50 g of water in the copper can and <u>record its temperature</u>.
2) <u>Weigh the spirit burner</u> and lid.
3) Put the spirit burner underneath the can, and light the wick. Heat the water, <u>stirring constantly</u>, until the temperature reaches about <u>50 °C</u>.
4) <u>Put out the flame</u> using the burner lid, and measure the <u>final temperature</u> of the water.
5) <u>Weigh</u> the spirit burner and lid <u>again</u>.

<u>Example: to work out the energy per gram of methylated spirit (meths):</u>

1) Mass of spirit burner + lid before heating = 68.75 g
2) Mass of spirit burner + lid after heating = 67.85 g → Mass of meths burnt = 0.9 g
3) Temperature of water in copper can before heating = 21.5 °C
4) Temperature of water in copper can after heating = 52.5 °C → Temperature change in 50 g of water due to heating = 31.0 °C
5) So 0.9 g of fuel produces enough energy to heat up 50 g of water by 31 °C.
6) It takes 4.2 joules of energy to heat up 1 g of water by 1 °C. This is known as the specific heat capacity of water.

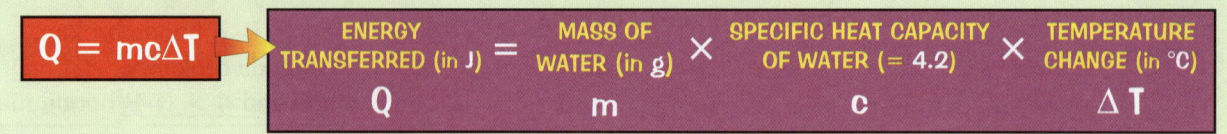

Energy is usually measured in joules (J) or kilojoules (kJ). 1 kJ is equal to 1000 J.

You'll be told this in the exam.

$Q = mc\Delta T$

ENERGY TRANSFERRED (in J)	=	MASS OF WATER (in g)	×	SPECIFIC HEAT CAPACITY OF WATER (= 4.2)	×	TEMPERATURE CHANGE (in °C)
Q		m		c		ΔT

7) Therefore, the energy produced in this experiment = 50 × 4.2 × 31 = <u>6510 joules</u>.
8) So 0.9 g of meths produces 6510 joules of energy...
   ... meaning 1 g of meths produces 6510/0.9 = 7233 J or 7.233 kJ
   — so meths contains <u>7.233 kJ/g</u>

Energy's wasted heating the can, air, etc. — so this figure will often be much lower than the actual energy content.

Section Seven — Energy and Equilibria

Equilibrium and Yield

> A reversible reaction is one where the products of the reaction can themselves react to produce the original reactants
>
> A + B ⇌ C + D

In other words, the reaction can go both ways.

Reversible Reactions Will Reach Equilibrium

1) If a reversible reaction takes place in a closed system then a state of equilibrium will always be reached.
2) Equilibrium means that the amounts of reactants and products will reach a certain balance and stay there. (A 'closed system' just means that none of the reactants or products can escape.)
3) The reactions are still taking place in both directions, but the overall effect is nil because the forward and reverse reactions cancel each other out. The reactions are taking place at exactly the same rate in both directions.

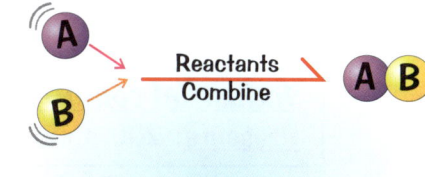

Changing Temperature and Pressure to Get More Product

1) In a reversible reaction the 'position of equilibrium' (the relative amounts of reactants and products) depends very strongly on the temperature and pressure surrounding the reaction.
2) If you deliberately alter the temperature and pressure you can move the 'position of equilibrium' to give more product and less reactants.

Temperature

All reactions are exothermic in one direction and endothermic in the other.

If you raise the temperature, the equilibrium position will shift towards the endothermic reaction to use up the extra heat and oppose this change. This means the yield of the endothermic reaction will increase and the yield of the exothermic reaction will decrease.

If you reduce the temperature, the equilibrium position will shift towards the exothermic reaction to produce more heat and oppose this change. This means the yield of the exothermic reaction will increase and the yield of the endothermic reaction will decrease.

Pressure

Many reactions have a greater volume on one side, either of products or reactants (greater volume means there are more gas molecules and less volume means there are fewer gas molecules).

If you raise the pressure it will encourage the reaction which produces less volume.

If you lower the pressure it will encourage the reaction which produces more volume.

Adding a CATALYST doesn't change the equilibrium position:

1) Catalysts speed up both the forward and backward reactions by the same amount.
2) So, adding a catalyst means the reaction reaches equilibrium quicker, but you end up with the same amount of product as you would without the catalyst.

Reversible reactions — double the fun...

Changing the temperature always changes the equilibrium position, but that's not true of pressure. If your reaction has the same number of gas molecules on each side of the equation, changing the pressure won't make any difference at all to the equilibrium position (it still affects the rate of reaction though).

Section Seven — Energy and Equilibria

The Haber Process

This is an important industrial process. It produces ammonia (NH_3), which is used to make fertilisers.

Nitrogen and Hydrogen Are Needed to Make Ammonia

nitrogen + hydrogen ⇌ ammonia (+ heat) $N_{2(g)} + 3H_{2(g)} \rightleftharpoons 2NH_{3(g)}$ (+ heat)

1) The nitrogen is obtained easily from the air, which is 78% nitrogen (and 21% oxygen).
2) The hydrogen comes from natural gas or from other sources like crude oil.
3) Some of the nitrogen and hydrogen reacts to form ammonia. Because the reaction is reversible — it occurs in both directions — ammonia breaks down again into nitrogen and hydrogen. The reaction reaches an equilibrium.

These gases are first purified.

Industrial conditions:
Pressure: 200 atmospheres;   Temperature: 450 °C;   Catalyst: Iron

The Reaction is Reversible, So There's a Compromise to be Made:

1) Higher pressures favour the forward reaction (since there are four molecules of gas on the left-hand side, for every two molecules on the right — see the equation above).
2) So the pressure is set as high as possible to give the best % yield, without making the plant too expensive to build (it'd be too expensive to build a plant that'd stand pressures of over 1000 atmospheres, for example). Hence the 200 atmospheres operating pressure.
3) The forward reaction is exothermic, which means that increasing the temperature will actually move the equilibrium the wrong way — away from ammonia and towards N_2 and H_2. So the yield of ammonia would be greater at lower temperatures.
4) The trouble is, lower temperatures mean a lower rate of reaction. So what they do is increase the temperature anyway, to get a much faster rate of reaction.
5) The 450 °C is a compromise between maximum yield and speed of reaction. It's better to wait just 20 seconds for a 10% yield than to have to wait 60 seconds for a 20% yield.
6) The ammonia is formed as a gas but as it cools in the condenser it liquefies and is removed.
7) The unused hydrogen (H_2) and nitrogen (N_2) are recycled so nothing is wasted.

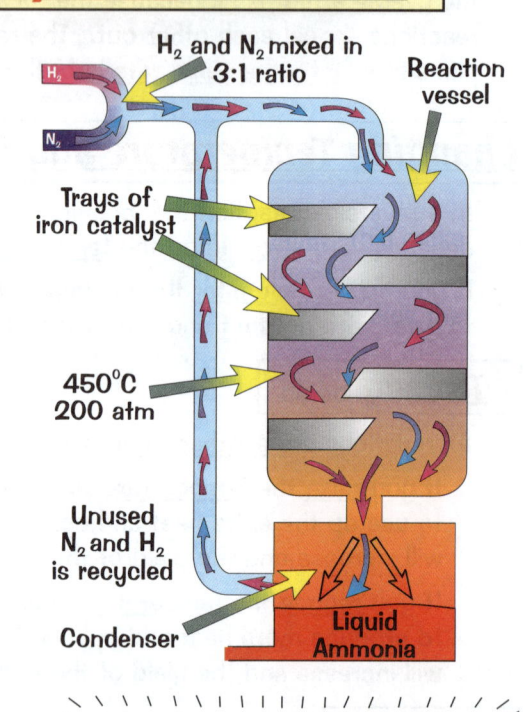

It's important to consider temperature, pressure and rate of reaction when working out optimum conditions for industrial processes such as the Haber process.

The Iron Catalyst Speeds Up the Reaction and Keeps Costs Down

1) The iron catalyst makes the reaction go faster, which gets it to the equilibrium proportions more quickly. But remember, the catalyst doesn't affect the position of equilibrium (i.e. the % yield).
2) Without the catalyst the temperature would have to be raised even further to get a quick enough reaction, and that would reduce the % yield even further. So the catalyst is very important.

You need to learn this stuff — go on, Haber go at it...

The trickiest bit is remembering that the temperature is raised not for a better equilibrium, but for speed. It doesn't matter that the percentage yield is low, because the hydrogen and nitrogen are recycled. Cover the page and scribble down as much as you can remember, then check, and try again.

Section Seven — Energy and Equilibria

Revision Summary for Section Seven

Well, I don't think that was too bad, was it... Reactions can be endothermic or exothermic, and quite a few of them are reversible. Energy changes are called enthalpy changes and you can work these out using a handful of numbers. And it was all rounded off with equilibria and the Haber process... Easy. Ahem. Well you know what's coming next... See what you know by testing yourself with the questions below. Anything you don't know, go back and look it up — it's the only way to learn.

1) Is energy released when bonds are formed or when bonds are broken?
2) What is an exothermic reaction?
3) What is an endothermic reaction?
4) What does ΔH stand for?
5) Values of ΔH can be negative or positive. What does this indicate?
6) Give three examples of exothermic reactions.
7) Give one application of an endothermic reaction.
8) The reaction to split ammonium chloride into ammonia and hydrogen chloride is endothermic. What can you say for certain about the reverse reaction?
9) a) Draw energy level diagrams for exothermic and endothermic reactions.
   b) Explain how bond breaking and forming relate to these diagrams.
10) What is the activation energy for a reaction? Mark it on your exothermic energy level diagram from Q9.
11) How does a catalyst affect: a) activation energy, b) overall energy change for a reaction?
12) a)* Calculate the energy change for the following reaction: $2H_2 + O_2 \rightarrow 2H_2O$
    You need these bond dissociation energies: H–H: +436 kJ/mol, O=O: +496 kJ/mol, O–H: +463 kJ/mol
    Hint: There are 2 O–H bonds in each molecule of water.
    b)* Is this an exothermic or endothermic reaction?
13) An acid and an alkali were mixed in a polystyrene cup, as shown to the right. The acid and alkali were each at 20 °C before they were mixed. After they were mixed, the temperature of the solution reached 24 °C.
    a) State whether this reaction is exothermic or endothermic.
    b) Explain why the cotton wool is used.

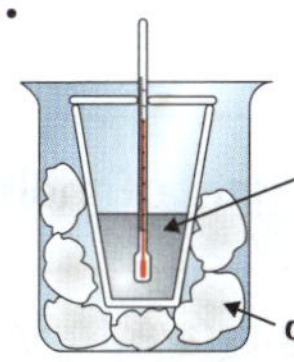

    20 cm³ of dilute sulfuric acid + 20 cm³ of dilute sodium hydroxide solution
    cotton wool

14) The apparatus below is used to measure how much energy is released when pentane is burnt. It takes 4.2 joules of energy to heat 1 g of water by 1 °C.
    a)* Using the following data, and the equation $Q = mc\Delta T$, calculate the amount of energy per gram of pentane.

Mass of empty copper can	64 g	Initial temperature of water	17 °C
Mass of copper can + water	116 g	Final temperature of water	47 °C

Mass of spirit burner + pentane before burning	97.72 g
Mass of spirit burner + pentane after burning	97.37 g

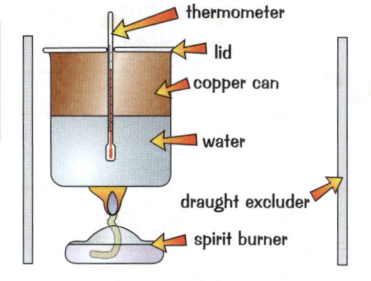

thermometer, lid, copper can, water, draught excluder, spirit burner

    b) A data book says that pentane has 49 kJ/g of energy. Why is the amount you calculated different?
15) What is a reversible reaction? Explain what is meant by equilibrium.
16) How does changing the temperature and pressure of a reversible reaction alter the equilibrium position?
17) Write the word equation for the Haber process.
18) State the industrial conditions used for the Haber process.
19) What determines the choice of pressure for the Haber process?
20) What determines the choice of operating temperature for the Haber process?
21) How is the ammonia gas produced by the Haber process converted into a liquid?

* Answers on page 94.

Section Eight — Electrolysis and Analysis

Electrolysis

Hmm, electrolysis. A not-very-catchy title for quite a sparky subject...

Electrolysis Means "Splitting Up with Electricity"

1) If you pass an electric current through an ionic substance that's molten or in solution, it breaks down into the elements it's made of. This is called electrolysis.
2) It requires a liquid to conduct the electricity, called the electrolyte.
3) Electrolytes contain free ions (ions that are free to move about). The ions are usually the molten or dissolved ionic substance.
4) In either case it's the free ions which conduct the electricity.
5) For the circuit to be complete, there's got to be a flow of electrons:
   - Negative ions move to the positive electrode (the anode), and lose electrons.
   - Positive ions move to the negative electrode (the cathode), and gain electrons.

   As ions gain or lose electrons they become atoms or molecules and are released.

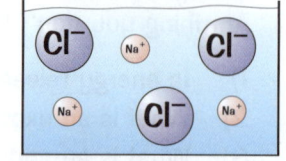

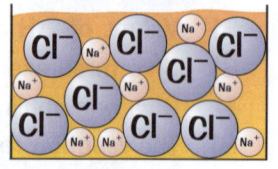

Electrolysis Reactions Involve Oxidation and Reduction

1) On page 34 you learnt about reduction involving the loss of oxygen. However...
2) Reduction is also a gain of electrons.
3) On the other hand, oxidation is a gain of oxygen or a loss of electrons.
4) So "reduction" and "oxidation" don't have to involve oxygen.
5) Electrolysis ALWAYS involves an oxidation and a reduction.

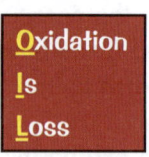

Oxidation Is Loss **Reduction Is Gain**

Remember it as OIL RIG.

Example:

The electrolysis of molten lead bromide

+ve ions move to the cathode (−ve electrode). Here they gain electrons (reduction). Lead is produced at the cathode.

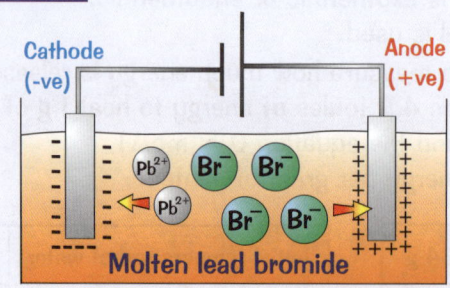

−ve ions move to the anode (+ve electrode). Here they lose electrons (oxidation). Bromine is produced at the anode.

The Half-Equations — Make Sure the Electrons Balance

Half equations show the reactions at the electrodes. The main thing is to make sure the number of electrons is the same for both half-equations. You need to make sure the atoms are balanced too.

For the electrolysis of molten lead bromide the half-equations are...

Cathode: $Pb^{2+} + 2e^- \rightarrow Pb$
Anode: $2Br^- \rightarrow Br_2 + 2e^-$
or $2Br^- - 2e^- \rightarrow Br_2$

... and for sodium chloride they would be:

Cathode: $Na^+ + e^- \rightarrow Na$
Anode: $2Cl^- \rightarrow Cl_2 + 2e^-$
or $2Cl^- - 2e^- \rightarrow Cl_2$

Faster shopping at the supermarket — use electrolleys...

Make sure you know the difference between oxidation and reduction, and which ions move to which electrodes. Electrolysis is used lots in real life, and it's nice to know how these things work, I say. Get ready for part two...

Electrolysis of Sodium Chloride Solution

As well as molten substances you can also electrolyse solutions. But first, a bit more about the products...

Reactivity Affects the Products Formed By Electrolysis

1) Sometimes there are more than two free ions in the electrolyte. For example, if a salt is dissolved in water there will also be some H^+ and OH^- ions. But you only get one product at each electrode.
2) At the cathode, the products depend on the reactivity of the elements present.
   - The more reactive an element, the keener it is to stay in solution as ions.
   - So if metal ions and H^+ ions are present, hydrogen is produced unless the metal is less reactive than it.
3) At the anode, the products depend on the reactivity of the ions present and also their relative concentration.
   - E.g. if low concentrations of OH^- and chloride (Cl^-) ions are present then oxygen will be formed from the OH^- ions, because the OH^- ions are slightly less reactive than the Cl^- ions.
   - But if OH^- ions and higher concentrations of Cl^- ions are present, then chlorine will be formed. This is because even though the chloride ions are a bit more reactive, there are loads more of them.

The Electrolysis of Sodium Chloride Solution

When common salt (sodium chloride) is dissolved in water and electrolysed, it produces three useful products — hydrogen, chlorine and sodium hydroxide.

H^+ ions are released from the water.

Even though OH^- ions are released from the water, Cl_2 is produced at the anode because there's a higher concentration of Cl^- ions.

Cathode (-ve) — flow of electrons

Anode (+ve) — flow of electrons

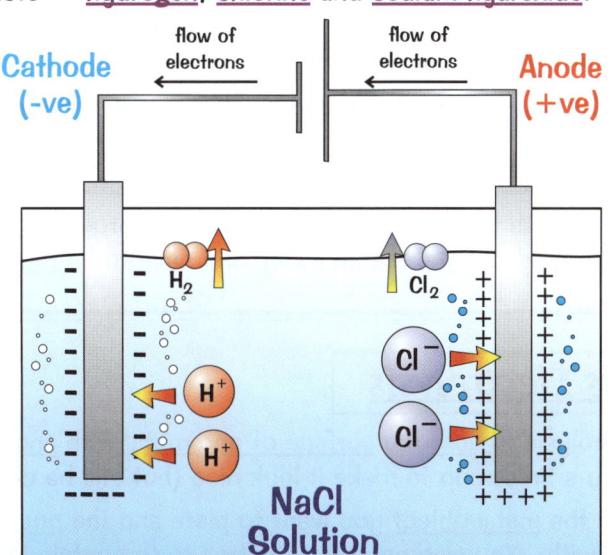

+ve ions move to the cathode (−ve electrode) and gain electrons (reduction). Hydrogen is produced at the cathode.

The half equation at the cathode is:
$$2H^+ + 2e^- \rightarrow H_2$$

−ve ions move to the anode (+ve electrode) and lose electrons (oxidation). Chlorine is produced at the anode.

The half equation at the anode is:
$$2Cl^- \rightarrow Cl_2 + 2e^-$$
or: $2Cl^- - 2e^- \rightarrow Cl_2$

1) At the cathode, two hydrogen ions accept two electrons to become one hydrogen molecule.
2) At the anode, two chloride (Cl^-) ions lose their electrons and become one chlorine molecule.
3) The sodium ions stay in solution because they're more reactive than hydrogen. Hydroxide ions from water are also left behind. This means that sodium hydroxide (NaOH) is left in the solution.

Useful Products from the Electrolysis of Sodium Chloride Solution

The products of the electrolysis of sodium chloride solution are pretty useful in industry.
1) Chlorine has many uses, e.g. in the production of bleach and plastics.
2) Sodium hydroxide is a very strong alkali and is used widely in the chemical industry, e.g. to make soap.

If only revision was made up of positive ions...

Electrolysis is brilliant for removing unwanted hair from your body. Good for women with moustaches, or men with hairy backs. And good for beauty clinics too — makes them some cash. Oh, wait, that's a different kind of electrolysis...

Electrolysis of Aluminium and Electroplating

I bet you never thought you'd need to know so much about electrolysis — but, sadly, you do.
So get reading this lot...

Electrolysis is Used to Remove Aluminium from Its Ore

1) Aluminium's a very abundant metal, but it is always found naturally in compounds.
2) Its main ore is bauxite, and after mining and purifying, a white powder is left.
3) This is pure aluminium oxide, Al_2O_3.
4) The aluminium has to be extracted from this using electrolysis.

Cryolite is Used to Lower the Temperature (and Costs)

1) Al_2O_3 has a very high melting point of over 2000 °C — so melting it would be very expensive.
2) Instead the aluminium oxide is dissolved in molten cryolite (a less common ore of aluminium).
3) This brings the temperature down to about 900 °C, which makes it much cheaper and easier.
4) However, a lot of energy is still needed for the process, as the temperature is still pretty high.
5) The electrodes are made of carbon (graphite), a good conductor of electricity (see page 30). 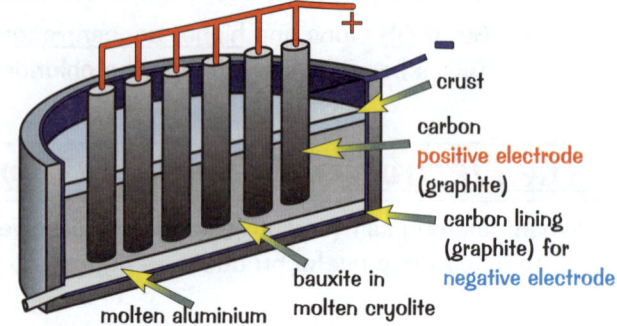
6) Aluminium forms at the negative electrode and oxygen forms at the positive electrode.

| Negative electrode: $Al^{3+} + 3e^- \rightarrow Al$ | Positive electrode: $2O^{2-} \rightarrow O_2 + 4e^-$ |

7) The oxygen then reacts with the carbon in the electrode to produce carbon dioxide. This means that the positive electrodes gradually get 'eaten away' and have to be replaced every now and again.

(Diagram labels: crust; carbon positive electrode (graphite); carbon lining (graphite) for negative electrode; bauxite in molten cryolite; molten aluminium)

Electroplating Uses Electrolysis

1) Electroplating uses electrolysis to coat the surface of one metal with another metal, e.g. you might want to electroplate silver onto a brass cup to make it look nice (but still be cheaper than a solid silver cup).
2) The negative electrode is the metal object you want to plate and the positive electrode is the pure metal you want it to be plated with. You also need the electrolyte to contain ions of the plating metal. (The ions that plate the metal object come from the solution, while the positive electrode keeps the solution 'topped up'.)

> **Example**: To electroplate silver onto a brass cup, you'd make the brass cup the negative electrode (to attract the positive silver ions), a lump of pure silver the positive electrode and dip them in a solution of silver ions, e.g. silver nitrate.

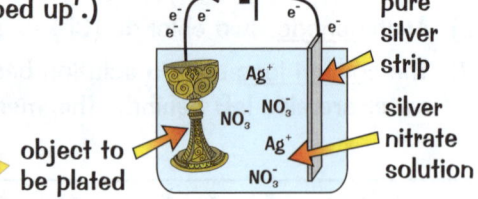

(Diagram labels: pure silver strip; silver nitrate solution; object to be plated; Ag^+, NO_3^-)

3) There are lots of different reasons for electroplating objects:
   - To improve their appearance — like our beautiful silver-plated brass cup.
   - To make them more durable.
   - To make them resistant to corrosion — e.g. steel car parts can be plated with chrome.
   - So that they conduct electricity — e.g conductive copper is used for electroplating in electronic circuits.

Silver electroplated text is worth a fortune...

There are loads of metals you can use for electroplating, but you just need to know about silver and copper plating. The tricky bit is remembering that the metal object you want to plate is the negative electrode and the metal you're plating it with is the positive electrode. Oh, and don't forget to learn about aluminium electrolysis.

Section Eight — Electrolysis and Analysis

Tests for Positive Ions

Forensic science involves a lot of chemical tests, which is what these next two pages are about. Before you start reading, you have to pretend you have a mystery substance. You don't know what it is, but you need to find out — just like that bloke off the telly who investigates murders.

If it's an ionic compound it'll have a positive and a negative part. So, first off, some tests for positive ions.

Flame Tests Identify Metal Ions

Remember, metals always form positive ions.

Compounds of some metals burn with a characteristic colour, as you see every November 5th when a firework explodes. So, remember, remember...

1) You can test for various metal ions by putting your substance in a flame and seeing what colour the flame goes.

   Lithium, Li^+, gives a crimson flame.
   Sodium, Na^+, gives a yellow flame.
   Potassium, K^+, gives a lilac flame.
   Calcium, Ca^{2+}, gives a red flame.
   Barium, Ba^{2+}, gives a green flame.

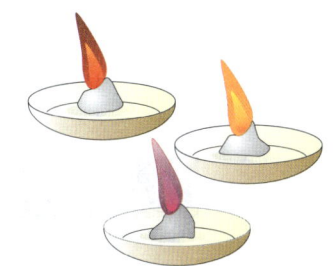

2) To flame-test a compound in the lab, dip a clean wire loop into a sample of the compound, and put the wire loop in the clear blue part of the Bunsen flame (the hottest bit). First make sure the wire loop is really clean by dipping it into hydrochloric acid and rinsing it with distilled water.

Some Metal Ions Form a Coloured Precipitate with NaOH

This is also a test for metal ions, but it's slightly more involved. Concentrate now...

1) Many metal hydroxides are insoluble and precipitate out of solution when formed. Some of these hydroxides have a characteristic colour.
2) So in this test you add a few drops of sodium hydroxide solution to a solution of your mystery compound — all in the hope of forming an insoluble hydroxide.
3) If you get a coloured insoluble hydroxide you can then tell which metal was in the compound.

"Metal"	Colour of precipitate	Ionic Reaction
Calcium, Ca^{2+}	White	$Ca^{2+}_{(aq)} + 2OH^-_{(aq)} \rightarrow Ca(OH)_{2(s)}$
Copper(II), Cu^{2+}	Blue	$Cu^{2+}_{(aq)} + 2OH^-_{(aq)} \rightarrow Cu(OH)_{2(s)}$
Iron(II), Fe^{2+}	Green	$Fe^{2+}_{(aq)} + 2OH^-_{(aq)} \rightarrow Fe(OH)_{2(s)}$
Iron(III), Fe^{3+}	Brown	$Fe^{3+}_{(aq)} + 3OH^-_{(aq)} \rightarrow Fe(OH)_{3(s)}$
Aluminium, Al^{3+}	White at first. But then redissolves in excess NaOH to form a colourless solution.	$Al^{3+}_{(aq)} + 3OH^-_{(aq)} \rightarrow Al(OH)_{3(s)}$ then $Al(OH)_{3(s)} + OH^-_{(aq)} \rightarrow Al(OH)_{4\;(aq)}^-$
Magnesium, Mg^{2+}	White	$Mg^{2+}_{(aq)} + 2OH^-_{(aq)} \rightarrow Mg(OH)_{2(s)}$

Testing metals is flaming useful...

Remember... your metal ion is your positive ion. To find out what your mystery ion is, start off with a flame test. If that doesn't give you any exciting colours, then go on and try the sodium hydroxide test. But don't forget that you can use a flame test or a precipitate test to identify calcium ions, although sadly you're looking for a different colour in each type of test. Looks like there's no easy way around it. I'd learn all the colours on this page and the metal ions they match up to — you might need any one of them in the exam.

Section Eight — Electrolysis and Analysis

Tests for Negative Ions

So now maybe you know what the positive part of your mystery substance is (see previous page). Now it's time to test for the negative bit.

Testing for Carbonates — Check for CO_2

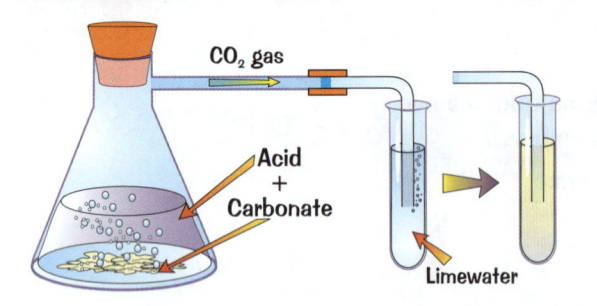

First things first — the test for carbon dioxide (CO_2).

1) You can test to see if a gas is carbon dioxide by bubbling it through limewater. If it is carbon dioxide, a white precipitate forms which turns the limewater cloudy.
2) You can use this to test for carbonate ions (CO_3^{2-}), since carbonates react with dilute acids to form carbon dioxide.

Acid + Carbonate → Salt + Water + Carbon dioxide

Tests for Halides and Sulfates

You can test for certain ions by seeing if a precipitate is formed after these reactions...

Halide Ions

To test for chloride (Cl^-), bromide (Br^-) or iodide (I^-) ions, add dilute nitric acid (HNO_3), followed by silver nitrate solution ($AgNO_3$).

A chloride gives a white precipitate of silver chloride.

$$Ag^+_{(aq)} + Cl^-_{(aq)} \longrightarrow AgCl_{(s)}$$

A bromide gives a cream precipitate of silver bromide.

$$Ag^+_{(aq)} + Br^-_{(aq)} \longrightarrow AgBr_{(s)}$$

An iodide gives a yellow precipitate of silver iodide.

$$Ag^+_{(aq)} + I^-_{(aq)} \longrightarrow AgI_{(s)}$$

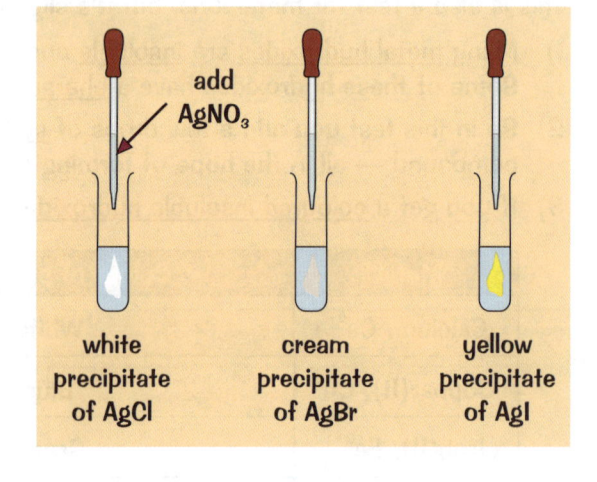

Sulfate Ions

1) To test for a sulfate ion (SO_4^{2-}), add dilute HCl, followed by barium chloride solution, $BaCl_2$.
2) A white precipitate of barium sulfate means the original compound was a sulfate.

$$Ba^{2+}_{(aq)} + SO_4^{2-}_{(aq)} \longrightarrow BaSO_{4(s)}$$

Sherlock never looked so good in a lab coat...

So you might have to do loads of different chemical tests to find out all the information about your mystery substance. It's a bit like detective work — eliminating suspects, narrowing down possibilities, and so on. It's the kind of stuff exam questions are made of, by the way, so be warned. They might give you the results from several chemical tests, and you have to say what the substance is.

Section Eight — Electrolysis and Analysis

Separating Mixtures

The components of mixtures <u>aren't</u> chemically joined — you can <u>separate</u> them <u>easily</u> with <u>physical methods</u>.

Mixtures are Easily Separated — Not Like Compounds

1) As you saw on page 64, a <u>mixture</u> is made up of two (or more) elements or compounds that <u>aren't chemically bonded</u> to each other. So, unlike in a compound, the parts of a mixture can be separated out by <u>physical methods</u> — see below for some examples.
2) The chemical properties of <u>each part</u> of the mixture <u>stay the same</u>. The <u>properties</u> of the <u>whole mixture</u> are just a <u>mixture</u> of the properties of the <u>separate parts</u>.
3) A <u>mixture</u> of <u>iron powder</u> and <u>sulfur powder</u> will show the properties of <u>both iron and sulfur</u>. It will contain grey magnetic bits of iron and bright yellow bits of sulfur.
4) <u>Air</u> is a <u>mixture</u> of gases (see page 33).
5) <u>Crude oil</u> is a <u>mixture</u> of different length hydrocarbon molecules (see page 64).

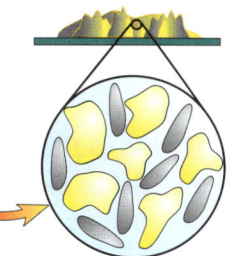

Iron and sulfur mixed together but unreacted

You need to know about these <u>three</u> methods for <u>separating</u> out mixtures:

1) Filtration is Used to Separate an Insoluble Solid from a Liquid

1) Filtration can be used if your <u>mixture</u> contains an <u>insoluble solid</u> and a <u>liquid</u>.
2) The mixture is poured into a <u>funnel</u> lined with <u>filter paper</u>. The liquid <u>passes through</u> the filter paper, leaving the solid behind.

Filter paper folded into a cone shape — the solid is left in the filter paper.

2) Crystallisation is Used to Separate a Soluble Solid from a Solution

1) <u>Crystallisation</u> can be used if your <u>mixture</u> contains a <u>soluble solid</u> and a <u>liquid</u>.
2) Pour the solution into an <u>evaporating dish</u>.
3) Slowly <u>heat</u> the solution. Some of the <u>liquid</u> will evaporate and the solution will get more <u>concentrated</u>. Stop heating when <u>crystals</u> start to form.
4) Remove the dish from the heat and leave it in a <u>warm place</u> for the rest of the liquid to slowly <u>evaporate</u> — this way you get nice <u>big crystals</u>.
5) Finally, you've got to <u>dry</u> the product — you can use a <u>drying oven</u> or a <u>desiccator</u> for this (a desiccator contains chemicals that remove water from the surroundings).

evaporating dish

3) Distillation is Used to Separate Out Liquids

1) <u>Distillation</u> is used to separate mixtures that contain <u>liquids</u>.
2) It works because <u>different liquids</u> have <u>different boiling points</u>.
3) The mixture is <u>heated</u>. The part of the mixture that has the lowest boiling point <u>evaporates</u>.
4) The <u>vapour</u> is then <u>cooled</u>, <u>condenses</u> (turns back into a liquid) and is <u>collected</u>.
5) The rest of the <u>mixture</u> is left behind in the flask.
6) You can use distillation to get <u>pure water</u> from <u>seawater</u>. The <u>water</u> evaporates and is condensed and collected. Eventually you'll end up with just the <u>salt</u> left in the flask.
7) With more equipment, you can carry out <u>fractional distillation</u> to separate out <u>more complicated mixtures</u> of liquids (see page 64).

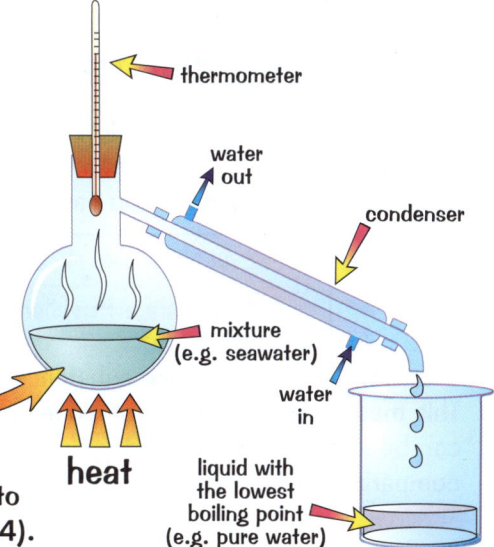

thermometer, water out, condenser, mixture (e.g. seawater), water in, heat, liquid with the lowest boiling point (e.g. pure water)

Revise mixtures — just filter out the important bits...

Remember that <u>mixtures aren't joined together chemically</u> — so <u>physical methods</u> will work a treat for separating them out. There are three separation techniques to know about — don't get them mixed up... geddit? (Groan.)

Section Eight — Electrolysis and Analysis

Paper Chromatography

Chromatography is another method used by chemists to separate out mixtures. You can use paper chromatography to separate out dyes — e.g. in inks, paints, food colourings etc. It's, er, fascinating stuff.

Chromatography Can Be Used to Identify Substances

You can use paper chromatography to identify different substances in a mixture. It uses the fact that different substances wash through wet filter paper at different rates.

1) Put spots of each mixture being tested on a pencil baseline on filter paper.
2) Roll up the paper and put it in a beaker containing a solvent, such as ethanol or water.
3) Make sure the dyes aren't touching the solvent — you don't want them to dissolve into it.
4) Place a lid on top of the container to stop the solvent evaporating.
5) The solvent seeps up the paper, taking the samples with it.
6) The different chemicals in the sample form separate spots on the paper. This is because some dissolve more readily in the solvent and travel more quickly up the paper.
7) The result of chromatography analysis is called a chromatogram. A chromatogram with four spots means there are at least four different substances in the sample mixture (e.g. four coloured dyes in black ink).

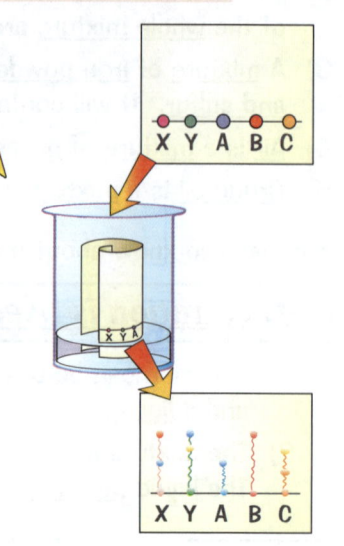

INTERPRETING A CHROMATOGRAM

One use for chromatography is to separate out the mixture of colouring agents in food. To identify which agents are present, run samples of known mixtures alongside the unknown mixture and compare where the spots end up.

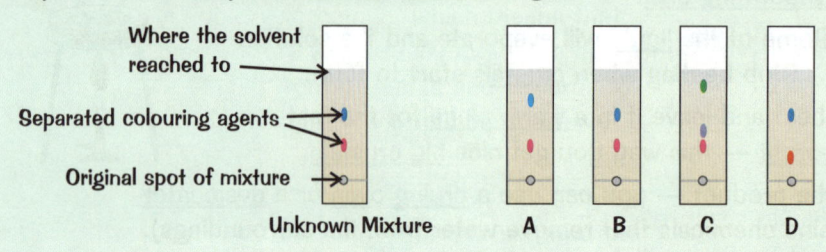

You can see from the position of the spots on the filter paper that the unknown mixture has the same composition as mixture B.

You can Calculate the R_f Value for Each Chemical

You need to know how to work out the R_f values for spots on a chromatogram.

An R_f value is the ratio between the distance travelled by the dissolved substance and the distance travelled by the solvent. You can find them using the formula:

$$R_f = \frac{\text{distance travelled by substance}}{\text{distance travelled by solvent}}$$

The R_f value of a particular substance is always the same. This means that unknown components in a mixture can be identified by measuring their R_f values and comparing them against known values.

So the R_f value for this chemical is B ÷ A.

Comb-atography — identifies mysterious things in your hair...

Always draw your baseline and write any labels in pencil not pen — the ink from the pen will dissolve in the solvent and confuse your results. Useful little tip that. Excellent.

Section Eight — Electrolysis and Analysis

Instrumental Methods

Nowadays there are some pretty clever ways of identifying substances using rather brilliant machines...

You Can Analyse Substances Using Machines

1) You can identify elements and compounds using instrumental methods — this just means using machines.

   Advantages of Using Machines
   - Very sensitive — can detect even the tiniest amounts of substances.
   - Very fast and tests can be automated.
   - Very accurate

2) One example of an instrumental method is gas chromatography linked to mass spectrometry (see below).

GC-MS Can be Used to Identify Substances

Gas chromatography can separate out a mixture of compounds and help you identify the substances present.

1) A gas is used to carry substances through a column packed with a solid material.
2) The substances travel through the tube at different speeds, so they're separated.
3) The time they take to reach the detector is called the retention time. It can be used to help identify the substances.
4) The recorder draws a gas chromatograph. The number of peaks shows the number of different compounds in the sample.
5) The position of the peaks shows the retention time of each substance.

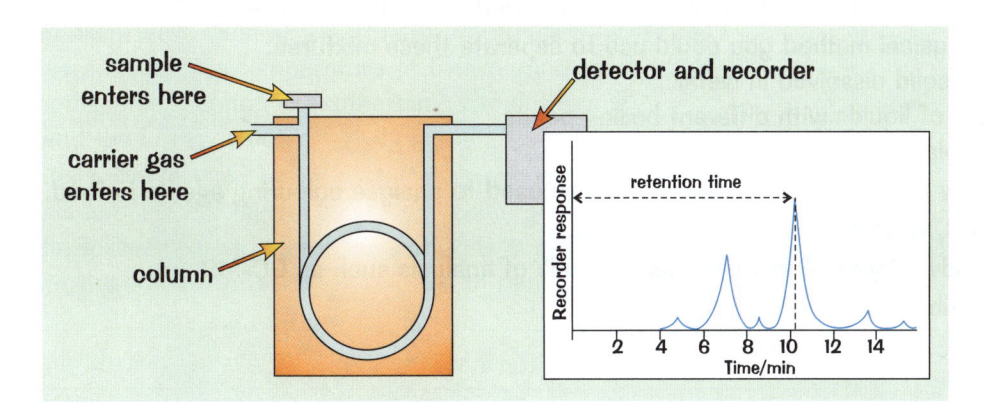

The gas chromatography column can also be linked to a mass spectrometer.

1) This process is known as GC-MS.
2) It can identify the substances leaving the column very accurately.
3) Like other instrumental methods, it's also very fast and can work with very small quantities of substances.
4) You can work out the relative molecular mass of each of the substances from the graph it draws. You just read off from the molecular ion peak.

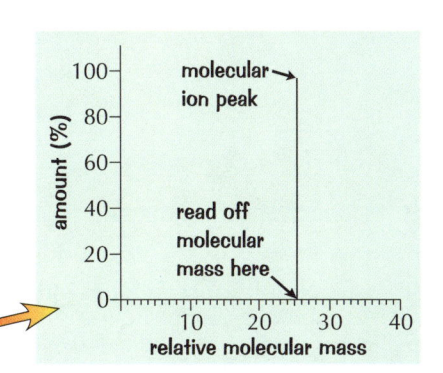

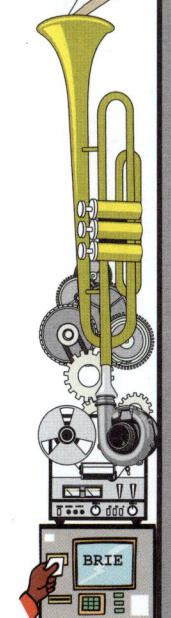

Unfortunately, machines can't do the exam for you...

Make sure you don't get gas chromatography muddled up with paper chromatography, and that you know what GC-MS stands for. Not, as you might think, giant curly-maned sheep. At least not in this context...

Section Eight — Electrolysis and Analysis

Revision Summary for Section Eight

Right. Here you go. One list of very important questions to test whether you've learnt this section properly. There's no backing out now — make sure you can answer each and every one of these questions, without any sneaky peeks. Or, indeed, if the question is on GC-MS, sneaky peaks. Top-notch chemistry joke there, folks — feel free to use that one yourself. Anyway, if you're struggling, go back through the section, have a browse and then try again. Repeat this until you can do them all perfectly. Have fun.

1) What is electrolysis? Explain why only liquids can be electrolysed.
2) In electrolysis, which electrode do the negative ions move to? What about the positive ions?
3) What does OIL RIG stand for?
4) Draw a detailed diagram with half equations showing the electrolysis of sodium chloride.
5) Give one industrial use of sodium hydroxide and two uses of chlorine.
6) Why is cryolite used during the electrolysis of aluminium oxide?
7) Write out the two half-equations for the reactions at the anode and the cathode in the electrolysis of aluminium.
8) Give two reasons for electroplating objects.
9) A forensic scientist carries out a flame test to identify a metal. The metal burns with a blue-green flame. Which metal does this result indicate?
10) What colour flame does potassium burn with?
11) What colour precipitate do iron(II) compounds form with sodium hydroxide?
12) What is the test for carbon dioxide?
13) How would you distinguish between solutions of:
    a) magnesium sulfate and aluminium sulfate,
    b) sodium bromide and sodium iodide,
    c) copper nitrate and copper sulfate?
14) Why can the components of a mixture be separated using physical methods?
15)* Name the physical method you could use to separate these mixtures:
    a) a soluble solid dissolved in water
    b) a mixture of liquids with different boiling points
    c) an insoluble solid mixed with a liquid
16) Describe how paper chromatography could be used to analyse colouring agents in food.
17) What is an R_f value?
18) Give three advantages of instrumental methods of analysis such as GC-MS.
19) Briefly describe how GC-MS works.

*Answers on page 94.

Index

A
accuracy 8
acid rain 35, 66
acids 53
activation energy 62, 78
air 33
alcohols 72
alkali metals 41
alkalis 53
alkanes 65, 68
alkenes 68–70
  test for 69
alloys 51
aluminium 86
ammonia 14, 29, 54, 82
amphoteric oxides 34
anode 47, 84, 85
anomalous results 8
atomic number 17
atoms 15

B
balancing equations 22
bar charts 9
barrier methods (to prevent rust) 38
bases 53
bauxite 86
bias 4
biodiesel 67
biofuels 67
bioleaching 48
bond energies 79
bromide ions (test for) 88
bromine 14, 42
bromine water 69
burning 34

C
calorimetry 80
carbon dioxide 67
  test for 58, 88
carbon monoxide 35, 66
carbonates 58
  test for 88
carboxylic acids 73
cast iron 50
catalysts 43, 62, 78, 82
cathode 47, 84, 85
chloride ions (test for) 88
chlorine 28, 37, 42, 85
chromatography 90
climate change 67
collision theory 61, 62
complete combustion 66
compounds 19, 26
concentration 55, 56
conclusions 11
condensation 13
control groups 7
copper
  extraction 47, 48
  properties 50
correlation 10, 11
covalent bonding 19, 28–30
cracking 68
crude oil 64, 65, 68
cryolite 86
crystallisation 89

D
data 9, 10
delocalised electrons 30, 50
dependent variables 6
designing investigations 6, 7
diamond 30
diffusion 14
displacement reactions 42, 45, 48
distillation 89

E
electrolysis 46, 47, 84–86
electrolytes 47, 84–86
electronic structures 18
electrons 15, 18, 26–29
electroplating 86
electrostatic attraction 27
elements 15, 40
empirical formulae 21
endothermic reactions 76–78, 81
energy level diagrams 78
energy levels (shells) 18
energy transfer 76, 80
enthalpy 76, 78, 79
environmental problems 49, 66, 67
equations 22
equilibrium 81
errors (in data) 8
esters 74
ethane 65
ethanoic acid 73
ethanol 67, 69, 72
ethene 69
ethyl ethanoate 74
evaluating investigations 12
evaporation 13
exothermic reactions 76–78, 81
explosions 59

F
fair tests 6
filtration 89
flame tests 87
fluoride 37
fluorine 42
formulae 19
fossil fuels 64-67
fractional distillation
  of air 33
  of crude oil 64
freezing 13
fuel cells 67
fuels 64-67, 72
fullerenes 31

G
gas chromatography 91
gases 13
giant covalent structures 30
giant ionic lattices 27
global dimming 67
global warming 67
graphite 30
groups (in the periodic table) 16, 40

H
Haber process 82
half-equations 84
halides 42
  test for 88
halogens 42
hazards 7
homologous series 65
hydrocarbons 64, 65, 68, 69
hydrogen 28, 67
  test for 44
hydrogen chloride 14, 29
hydroxides 54
hypotheses 2

I
independent variables 6
indicators 53
instrumental methods 91
intermolecular forces 30
iodide ions (test for) 88
iodine 42
ionic bonding 19, 26
ionic compounds 27, 84
ions 19, 26, 27
iron 38, 50
isotopes 17

L
landfill 71
lead bromide (electrolysis) 84
limestone 58
limewater 58, 88
line graphs 10
liquids 13
lithium 41
litmus paper 53

M
mass number 17
mass spectrometry 91
masses in reactions 23
means (averages) 9
melting 13
metal carbonates 58
metal extraction 46–49
metal hydroxides 54
metal ions (tests for) 87
metal oxides 54
metallic bonding 50
metals
  displacement reactions 45
  properties 50
  reactions with acids 44
  reactions with water 44
  reactivity 45
  structure 50
methane 28, 65
methanoic acid 73
methanol 72
methyl orange 53
methylated spirit 72
mixtures 89
models 2
moles 20
mystery substances 87, 88

N
nanoparticles 31
nanotubes 31
negative ions (tests for) 88
neutralisation 53–55, 77
neutrons 15
nitinol 51
nitrogen oxides 35
noble gases 16, 40
nucleus 15

O
OIL RIG 84
ores 46
oxidation 34, 38, 77, 84
oxides 34, 54
oxygen 29
  test for 33

P
partial combustion 66
percentage mass 21
percentage yield 24
perfumes 72, 74
periodic table 16, 40
pH scale 53
phenolphthalein 53
phytomining 48
pollution 35
poly(ethene) 70, 71
polymers 70, 71
positive ions (tests for) 87
potassium 41
potassium manganate(VII) 14
precipitation reactions 57, 60, 87
precision 8
predictions 2
propane 65
propanoic acid 73
propanol 72
propene 69
protons 15

R
rates of reaction 59–62
  measuring 60
reactivity series 45
recycling (metals) 49
reduction 34, 46, 84
relative atomic mass 17
relative formula mass 20
renewable fuels 67
repeatable results 3
reproducible results 3
reversible reactions 24, 77, 81, 82
R_f values 90
rust 38

S
sacrificial protection (from rust) 38
salts 54, 57
sample size 3
separating mixtures 89, 90
shape memory alloys 51
shielding (in atoms) 40
silicon dioxide 30
simple molecular substances 30
smart materials 51
sodium 41
sodium chloride (electrolysis) 85
sodium hydroxide 85
solids 13
solvents 72
states of matter 13
steel 51
sublimation 13
sulfate ions (test for) 88
sulfur dioxide 35, 66

T
thermal decomposition 58, 68, 77
thermosetting plastics 70
thermosoftening plastics 70
titrations 55, 56
transition elements 43
trial runs 7

U
universal indicator 53

V
validity 3
variables 6
vinegar 73

W
water 29
  filters 37
  quality 36, 37
  softeners 37
  test for 36
  treatment 36

Y
yield 24, 81

Answers

Bottom of page 20
1) Cu: 63.5, K: 39, Kr: 84, Cl: 35.5
2) NaOH: 40, Fe_2O_3: 160, C_6H_{14}: 86, $Mg(NO_3)_2$: 148

Bottom of page 21
1) a) 30.0% b) 88.9% c) 48.0% d) 65.3%
2) CH_4

Bottom of page 22
1) $Fe_2O_3 + 3H_2 \rightarrow 2Fe + 3H_2O$
2) $6HCl + 2Al \rightarrow 2AlCl_3 + 3H_2$

Bottom of page 23
1) 21.4 g
2) 38.0 g

Revision Summary for Section One (page 25)
8) a) Ca b) C c) Na
12) b) i) 40 ii) 108
17) b) i) 84 ii) 106 iii) 81 iv) 56 v) 17
19) moles = mass ÷ Mr
    = 147 ÷ (23 + 16 + 1)
    = 147 ÷ 40 = 3.7 moles (to 1 d.p.)
20) mass = moles × Mr = 0.05 × (24 + 16)
    = 0.05 × 40 = 2 g
21) a) i) 12.0% ii) 27.3% iii) 75.0%
    b) i) 74.2% ii) 70.0% iii) 52.9%
22) b) $MgSO_4$
23) a) $2Na + 2H_2O \rightarrow 2NaOH + H_2$
    b) $2Al + 6HCl \rightarrow 2AlCl_3 + 3H_2$
25) a) $4Na + O_2 \rightarrow 2Na_2O$
    4Na: 4 × 23 = 92
    $2Na_2O$: ((23 × 2) + 16) × 2) = 124

Na	Na_2O
92 g	124 g
1 g	1.348 g
50 g	67.4 g (to 1 d.p.)

    b) Percentage yield = 42.3 ÷ 67.4 × 100
    = 62.8% (to 1 d.p.)

Revision Summary for Section Two (page 32)
3) [diagram of Mg ion with 2+ charge]

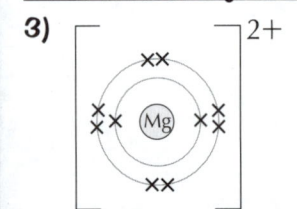

11) A: simple molecular, B: giant covalent, C: giant ionic

Revision Summary for Section Five (page 63)
11) a) No. of moles NaOH = 0.2 × (25 ÷ 1000)
    = 0.005
    $HCl + NaOH \rightarrow NaCl + H_2O$, so no. of moles HCl = 0.005
    Concentration HCl (moles per dm^3)
    = 0.005 ÷ (49 ÷ 1000)
    = 0.102 moles per dm^3
    b) M_r HCl = 1 + 35.5 = 36.5
    mass = number of moles × M_r
    = 0.102 × 36.5 = 3.72 grams per dm^3
21) b) [graph of Amount of gas evolved vs Time, showing Samples A, B, C, D]

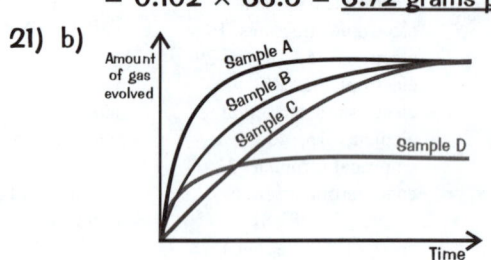

Revision Summary for Section Six (page 75)
5) Propane — the fuel needs to be a gas at −10 °C to work in a camping stove.

Revision Summary for Section Seven (page 83)
12) a) Bonds broken: 2 moles of H–H bonds
    = 2 × 436 = 872 kJ
    1 mole of O=O bonds = 496 kJ
    Total energy needed to break bonds
    = 872 + 496 = 1368 kJ
    Bonds made: 2 moles of (2 × O–H bonds)
    = 2 × 2 × 463 = 1852 kJ
    Energy change = 1368 − 1852 = −484 kJ/mol.
    b) This is an exothermic reaction.
14) a) Mass of water heated = 116 g − 64 g = 52 g
    Temperature rise of water = 47 °C − 17 °C
    = 30 °C
    Mass of pentane burnt = 97.72 g − 97.37 g
    = 0.35 g
    So 0.35 g of pentane provides enough energy to heat up 52 g of water by 30 °C.
    It takes 4.2 joules of energy to heat up 1 g of water by 1 °C.
    Q = mcΔT. Therefore, the energy produced in this experiment is 52 × 4.2 × 30 = 6552 J.
    So, 0.35 g of pentane produces 6552 J of energy... meaning 1 g of pentane produces 6552/0.35 = 18 720 J or 18.720 kJ, so pentane contains 18.270 kJ/g.

Revision Summary for Section Eight (page 92)
15) a) crystallisation
    b) fractional distillation
    c) filtration